My Food & Snacks Coloring Book
BOLD AND SIMPLE

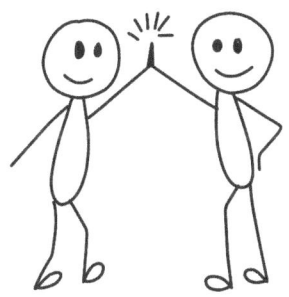

By

ARC

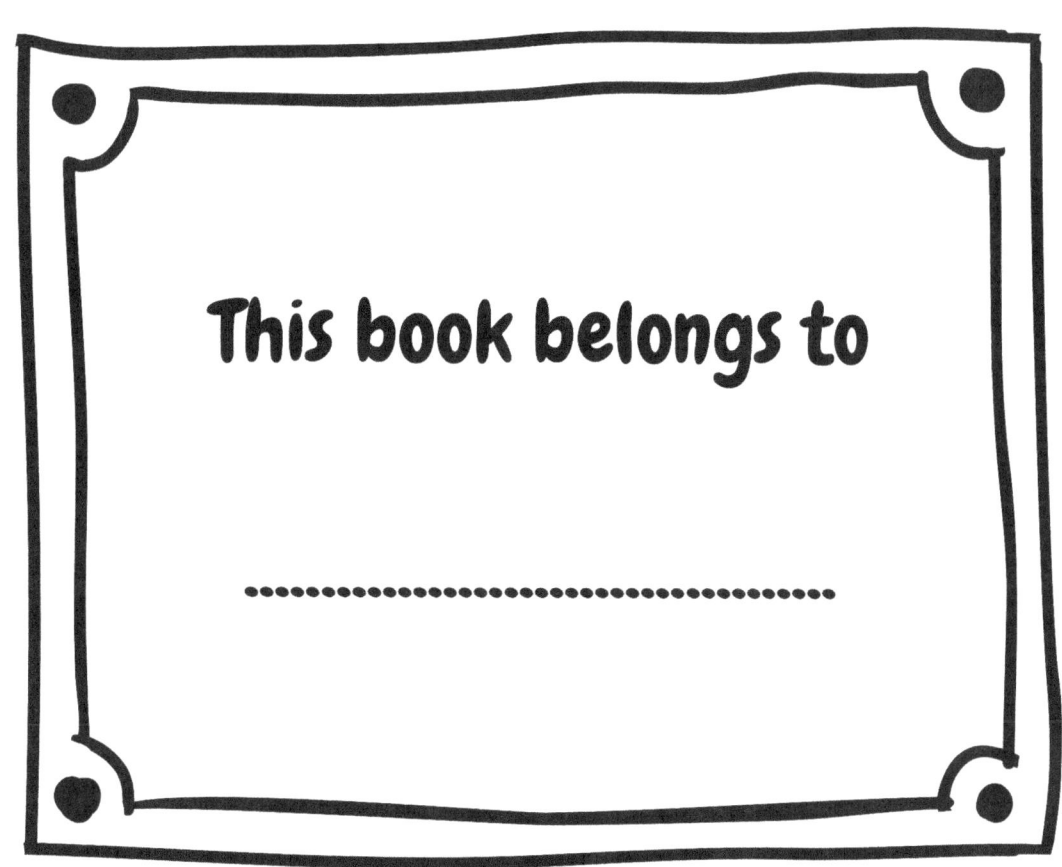

This book belongs to

....

Thank you for bringing this book into your life.
I hope each page adds a little joy and color to
your days. Cozy up with your favorite snacks,
and enjoy the journey!

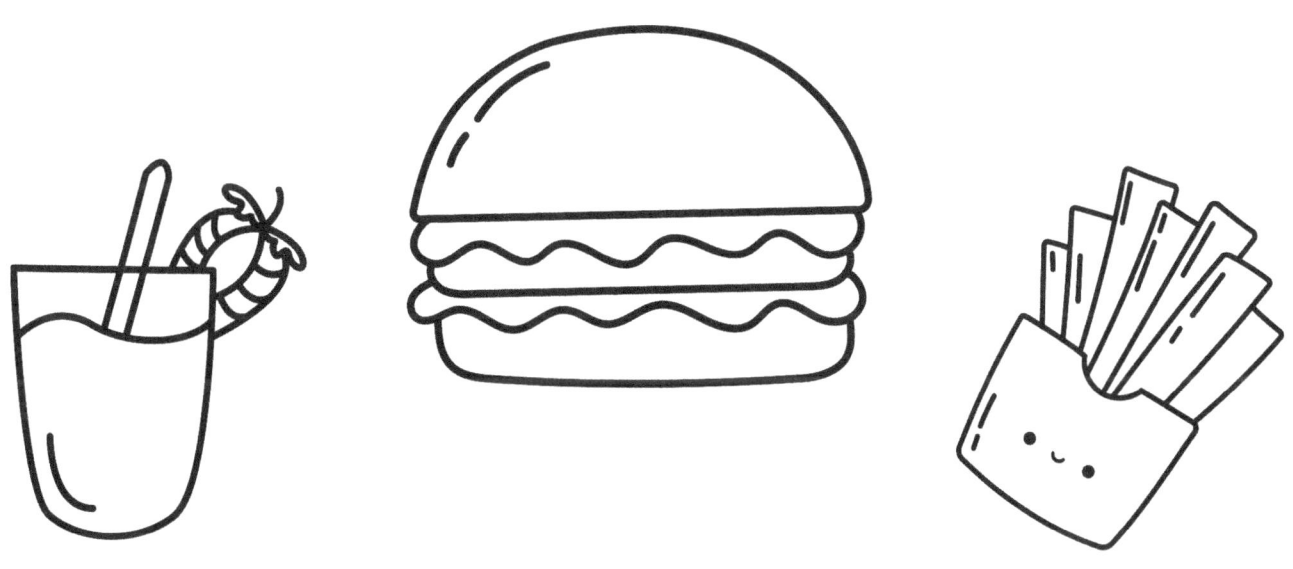

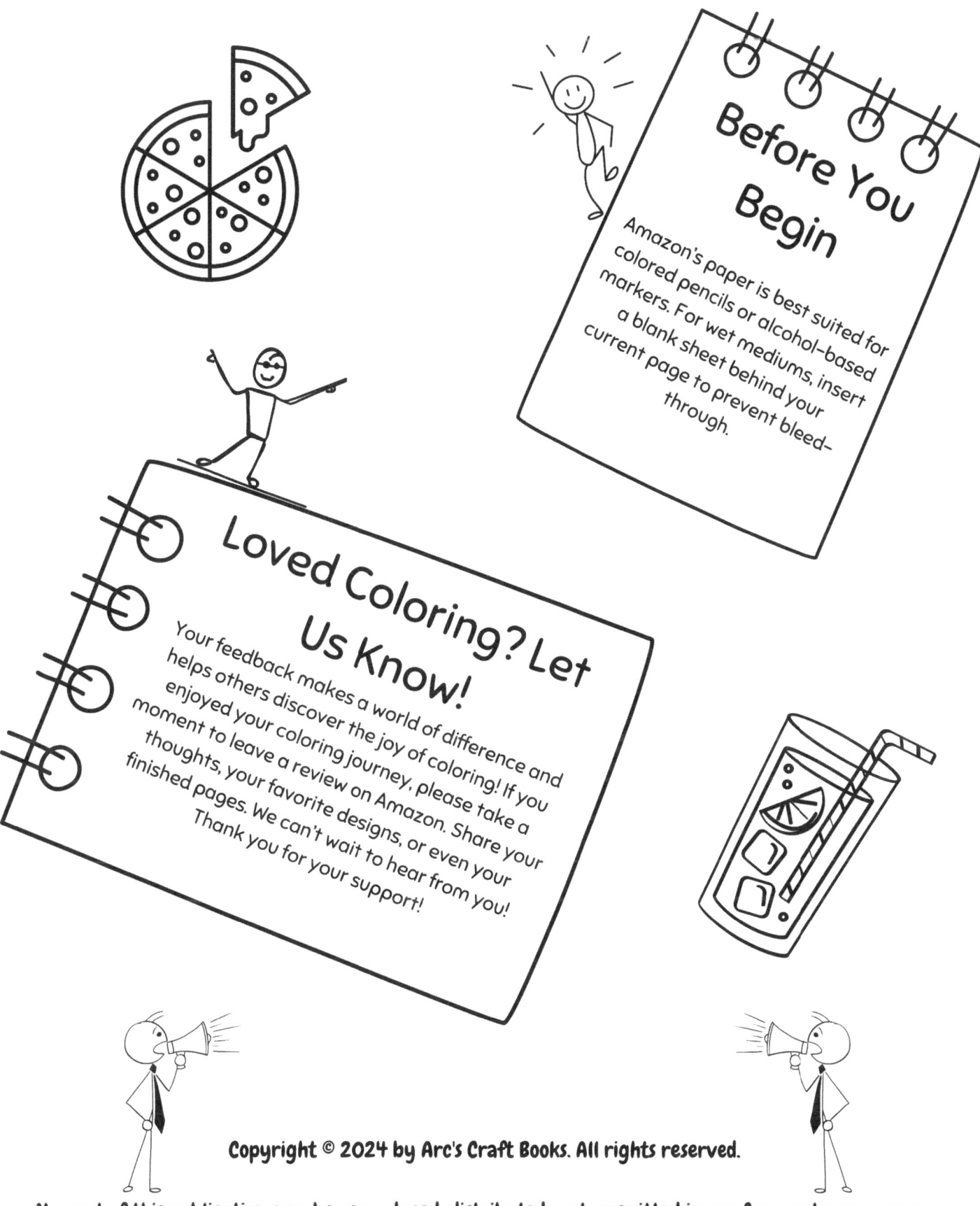

Before You Begin

Amazon's paper is best suited for colored pencils or alcohol-based markers. For wet mediums, insert a blank sheet behind your current page to prevent bleed-through.

Loved Coloring? Let Us Know!

Your feedback makes a world of difference and helps others discover the joy of coloring! If you enjoyed your coloring journey, please take a moment to leave a review on Amazon. Share your thoughts, your favorite designs, or even your finished pages. We can't wait to hear from you! Thank you for your support!

Copyright © 2024 by Arc's Craft Books. All rights reserved.

No part of this publication may be reproduced, distributed, or transmitted in any form or by any means, including photocopying, recording, or other electronic or mechanical methods, without the prior written permission of the publisher, except in the case of brief quotations embodied in critical reviews and certain other noncommercial uses permitted by copyright law.

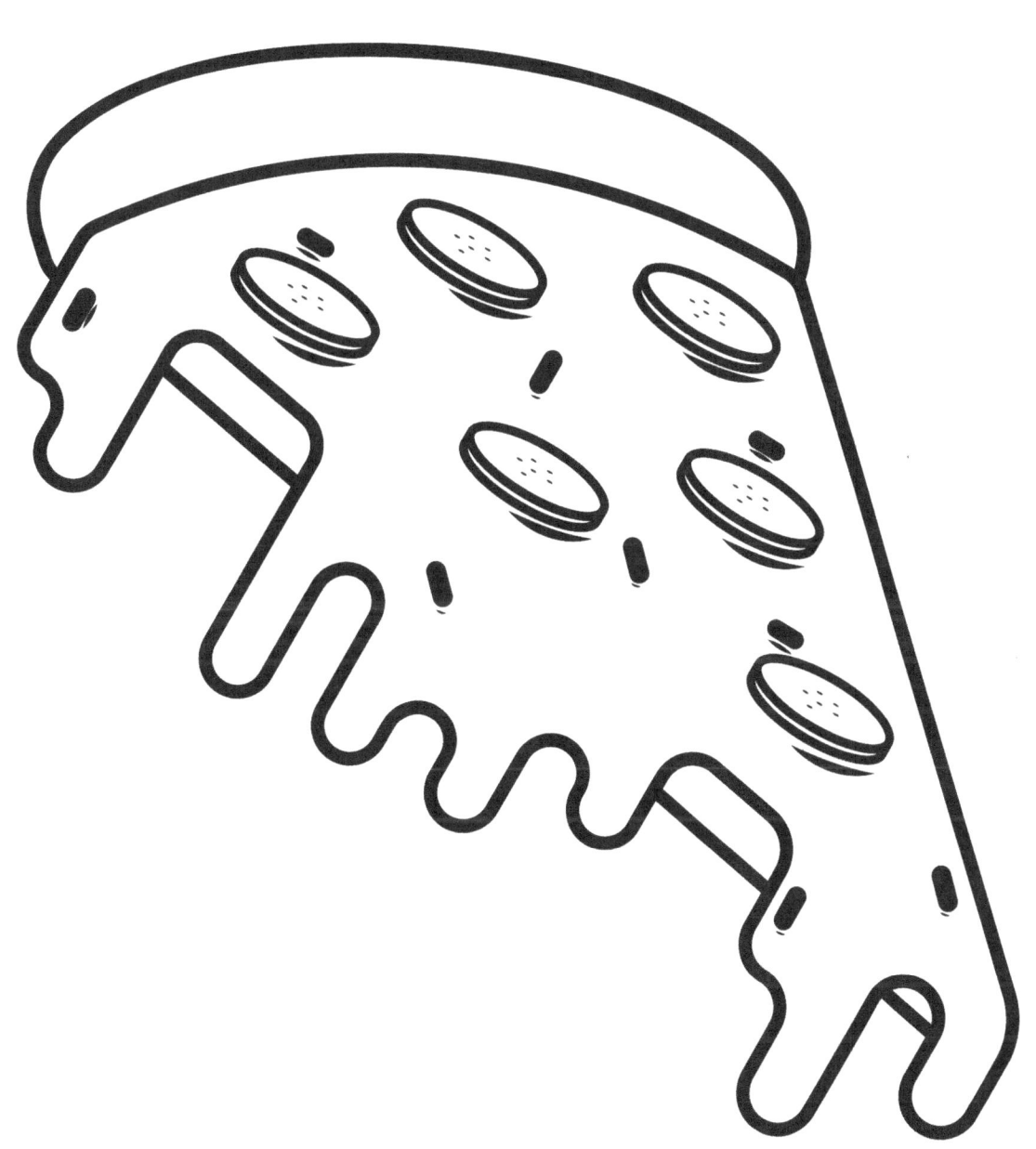

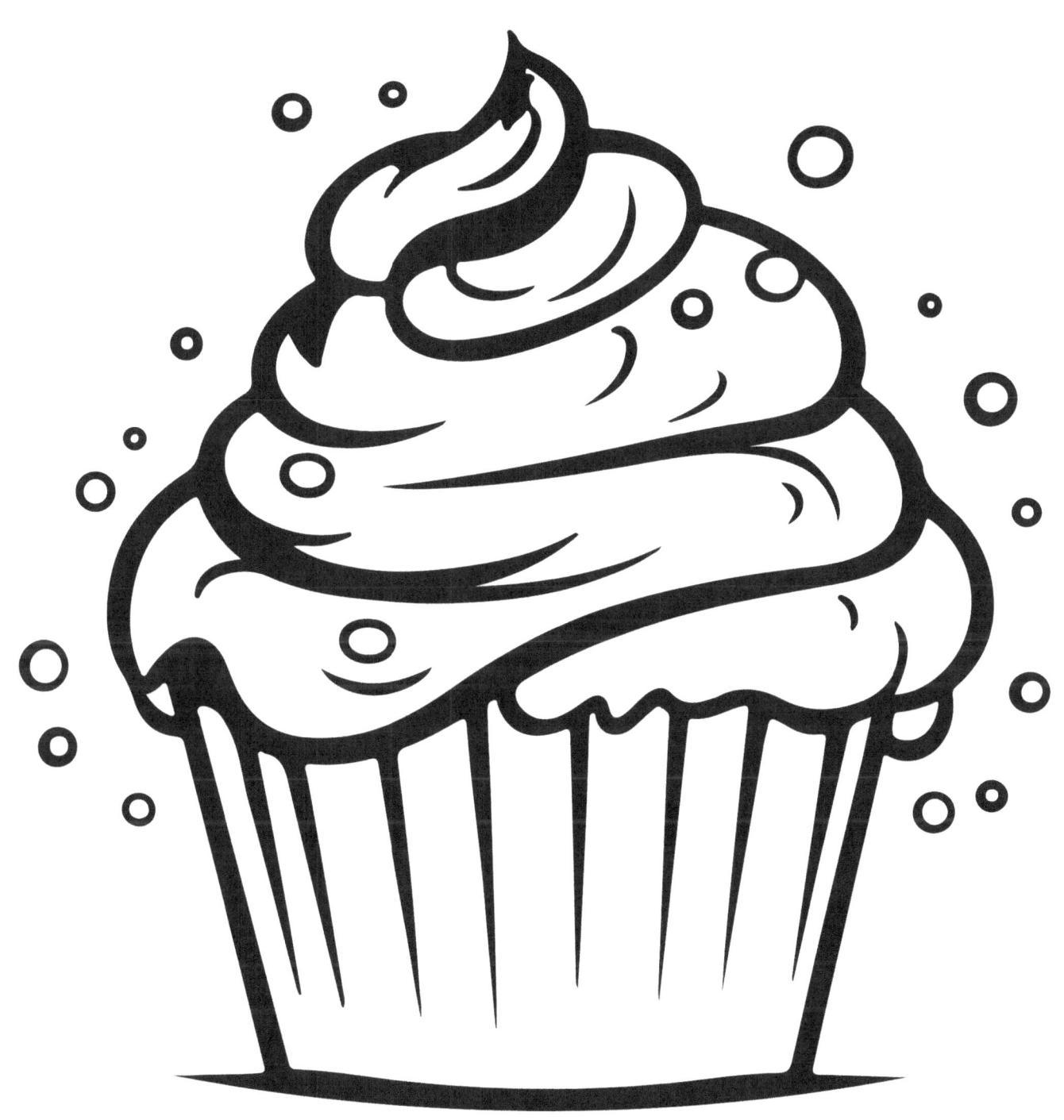

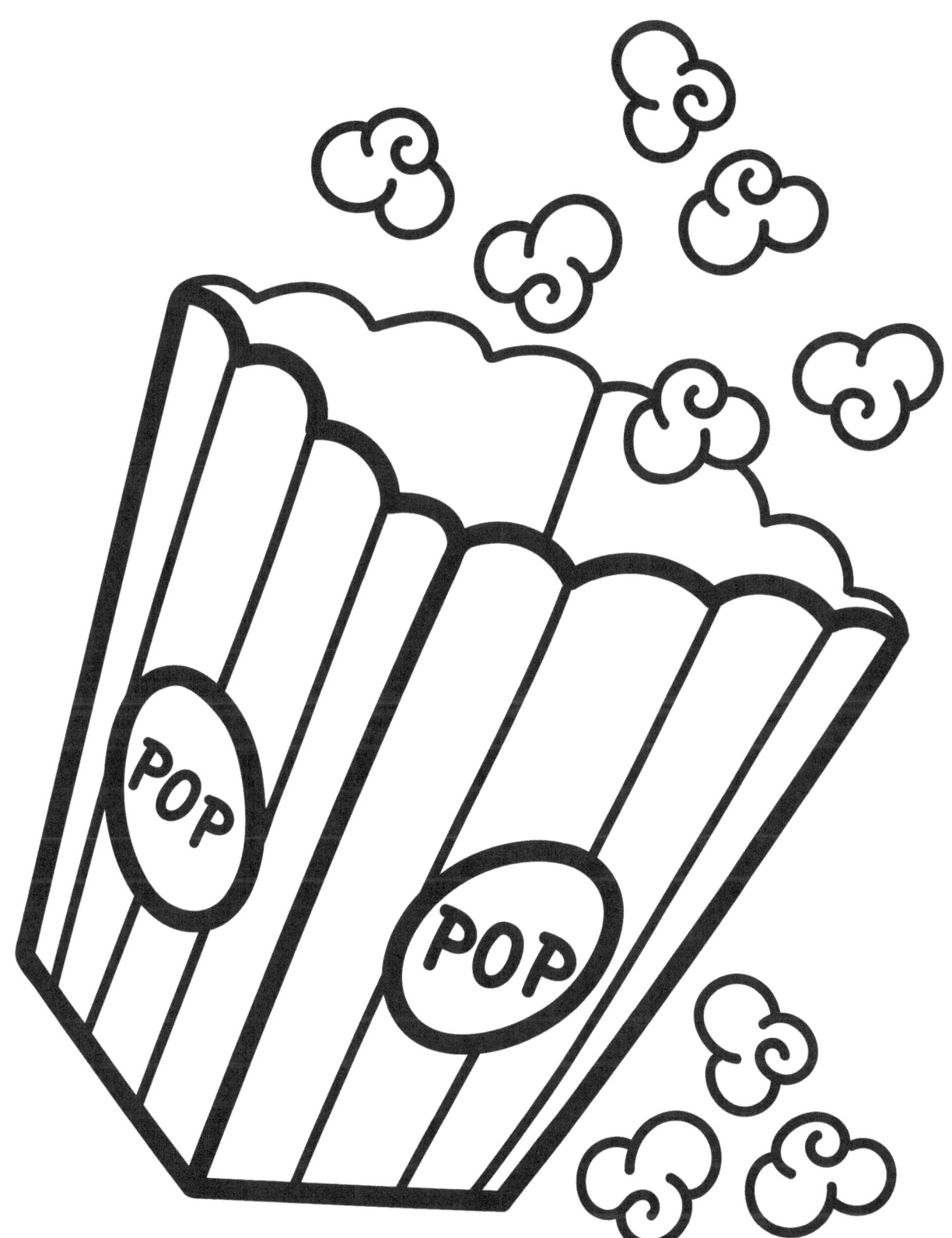

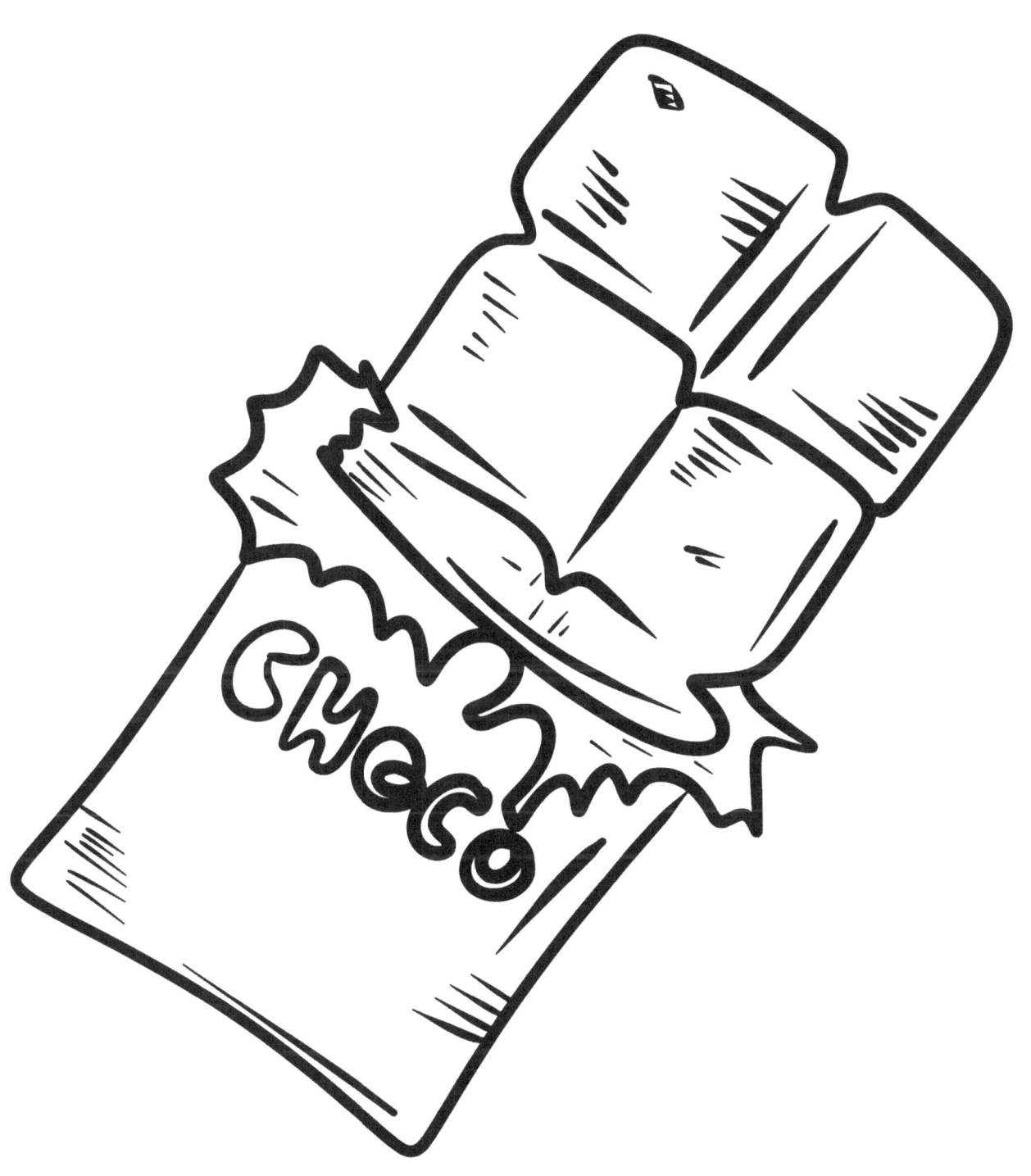

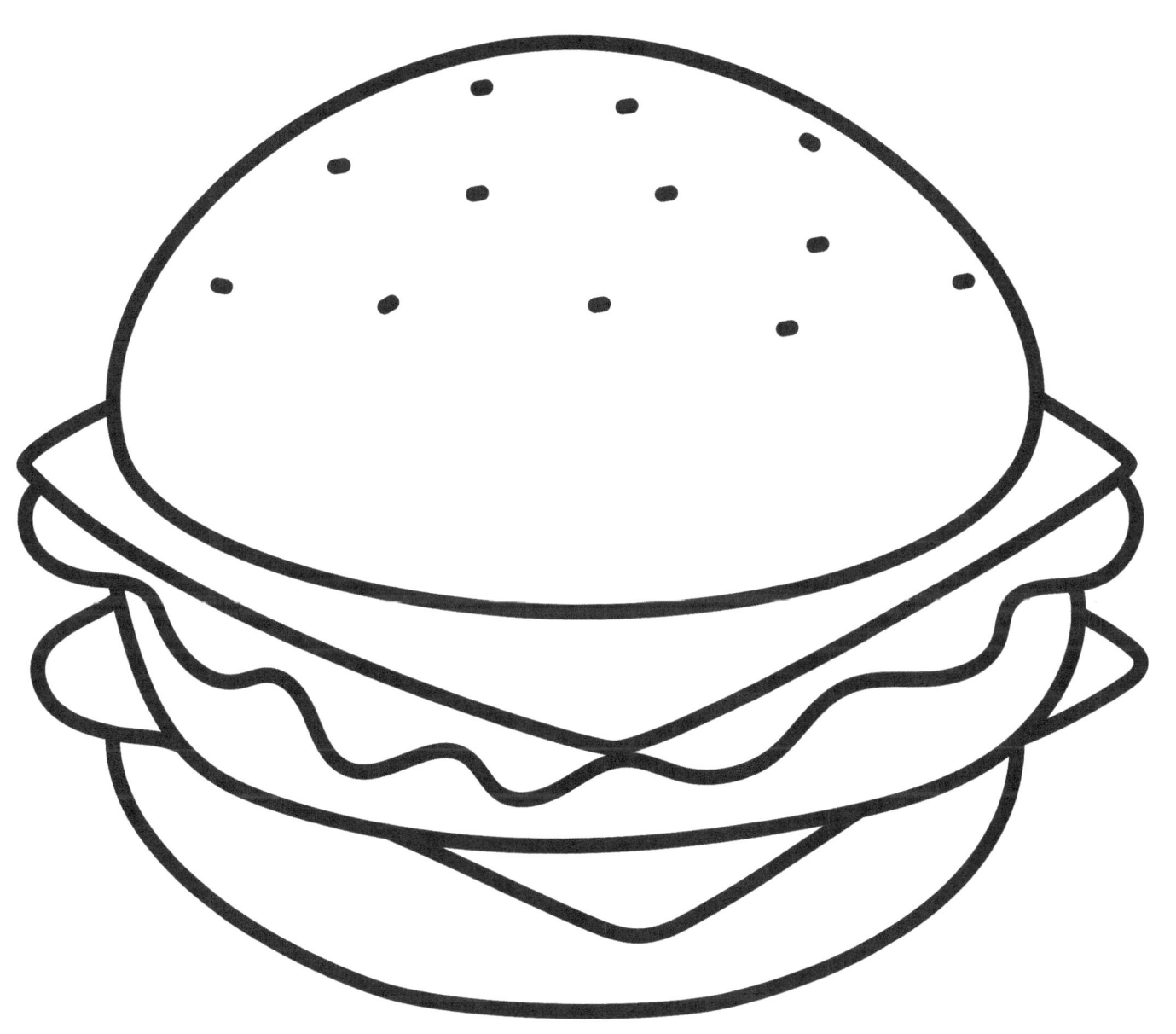

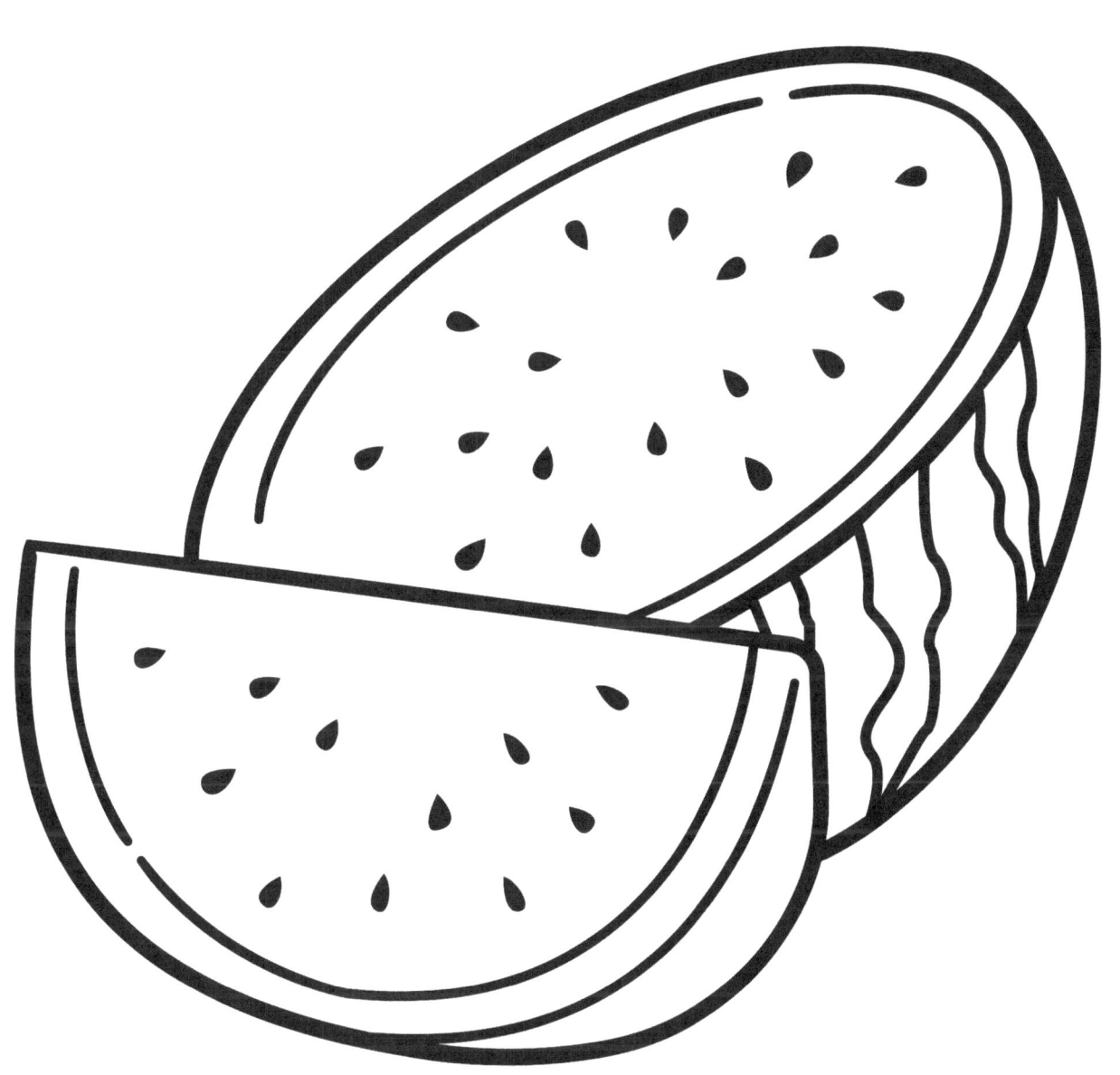

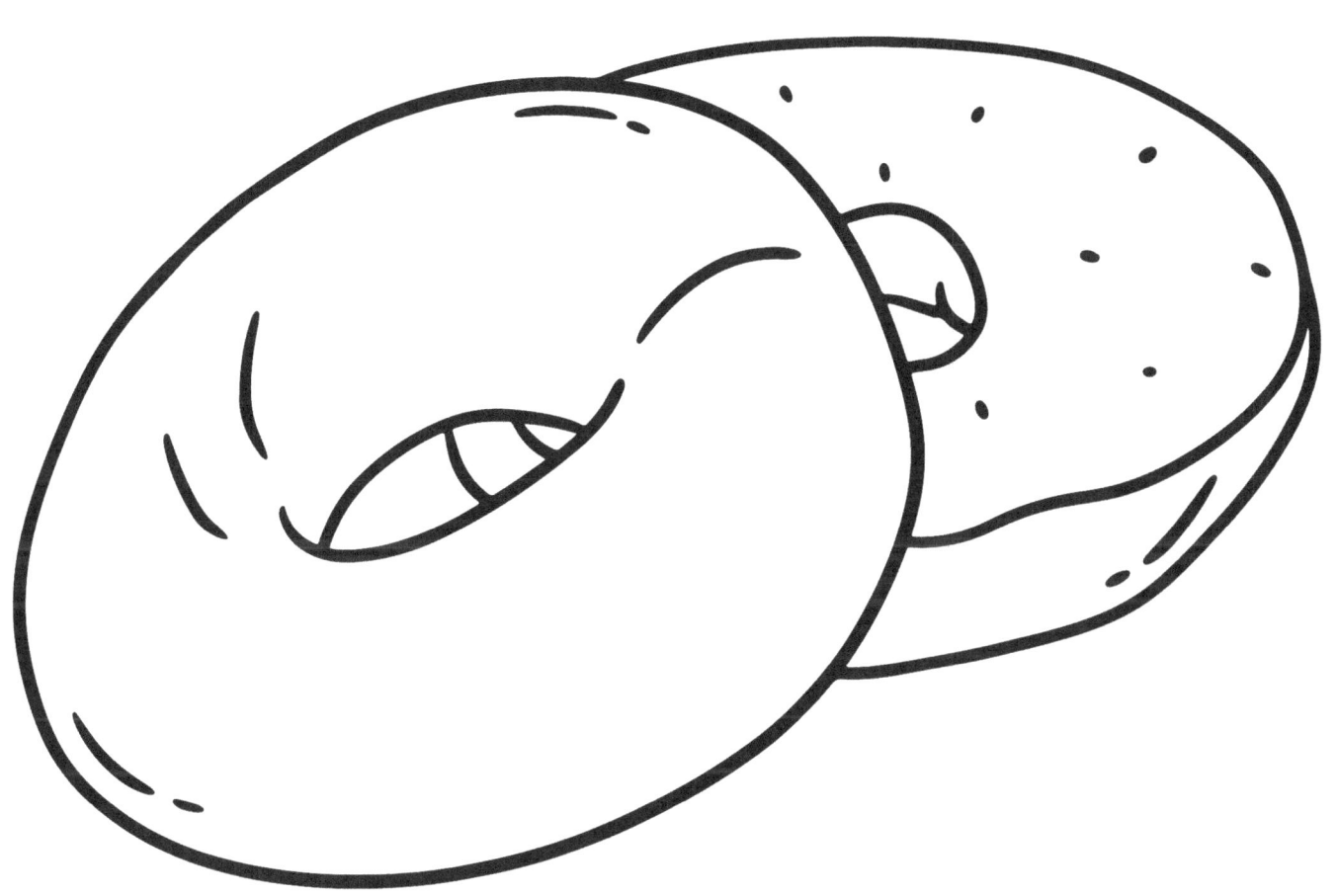

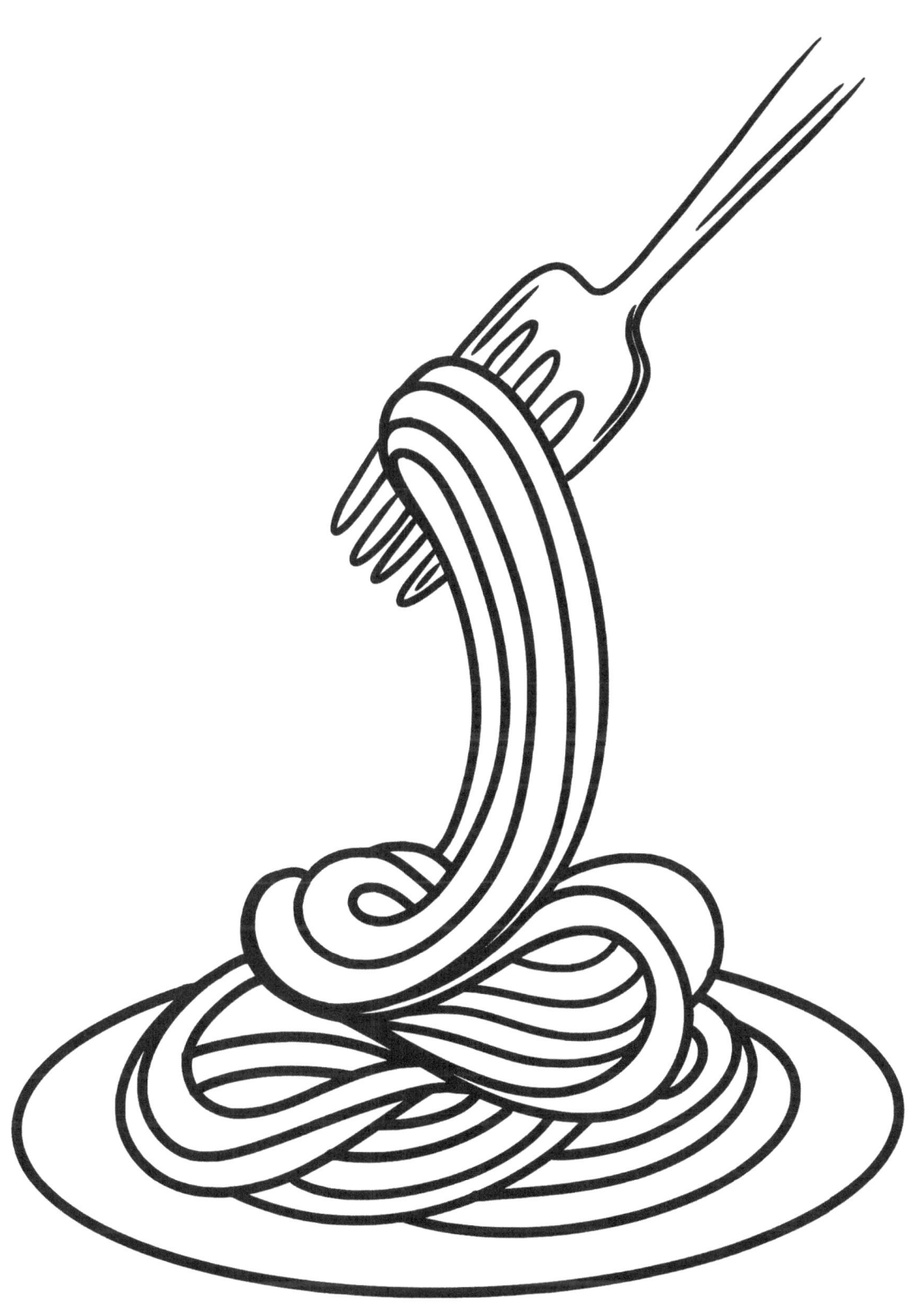

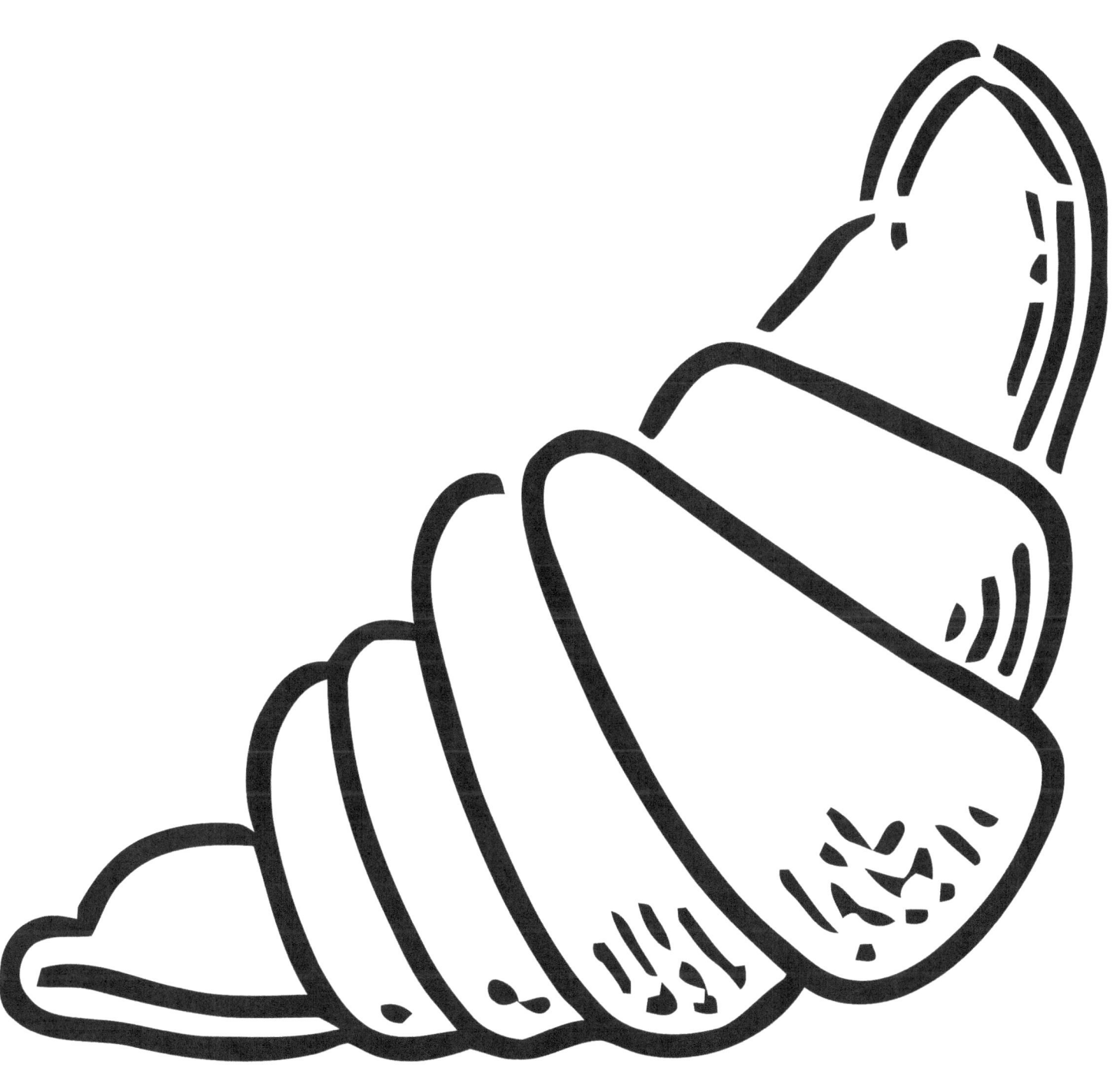

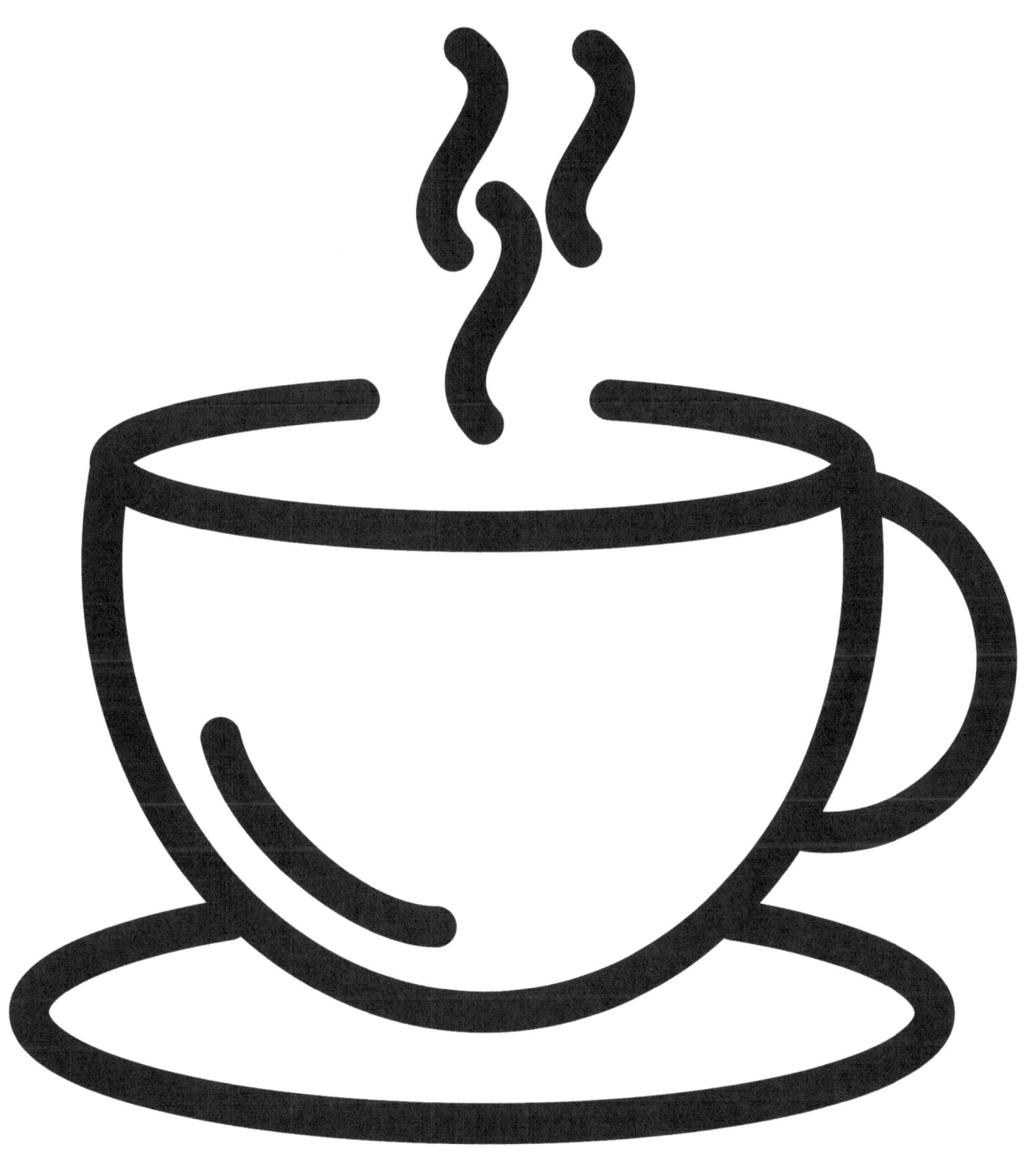

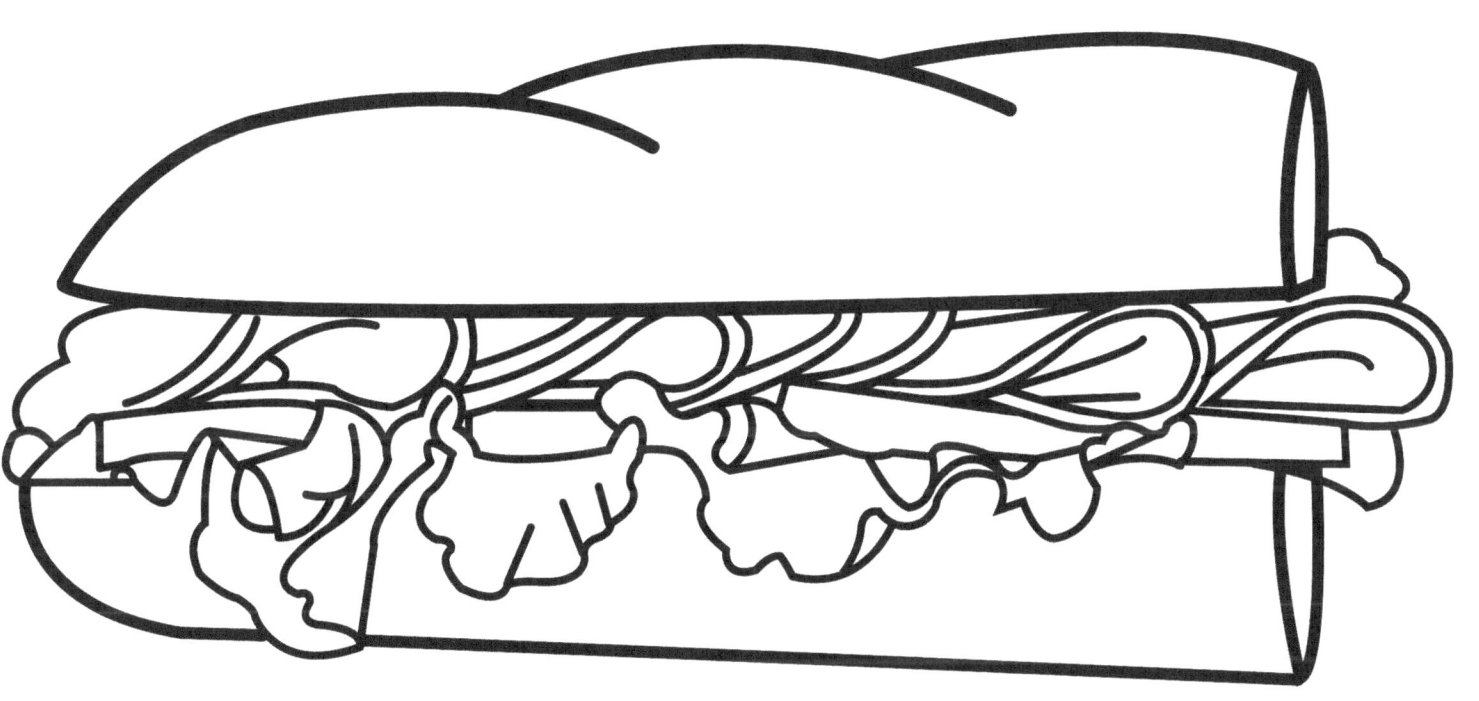

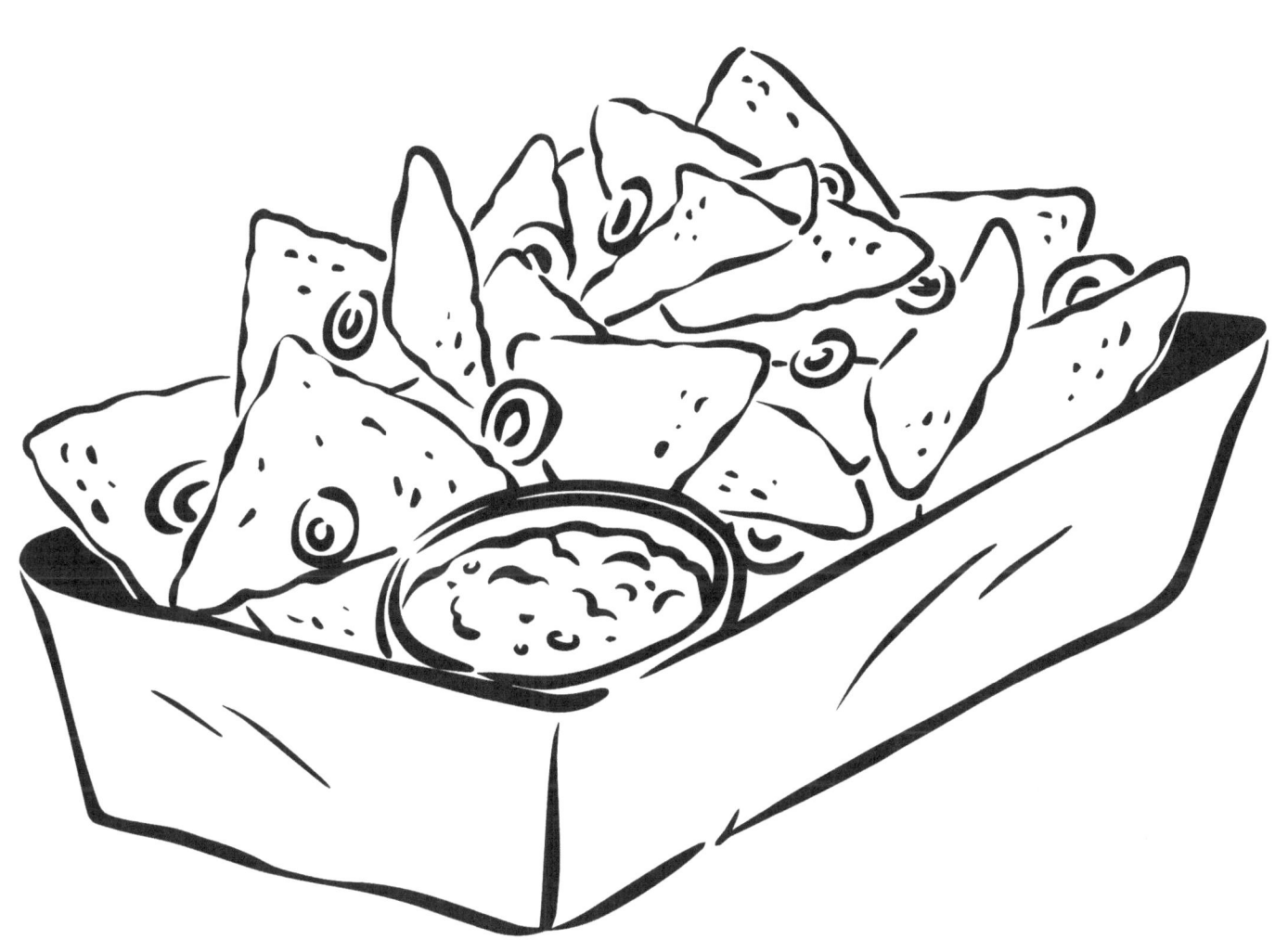

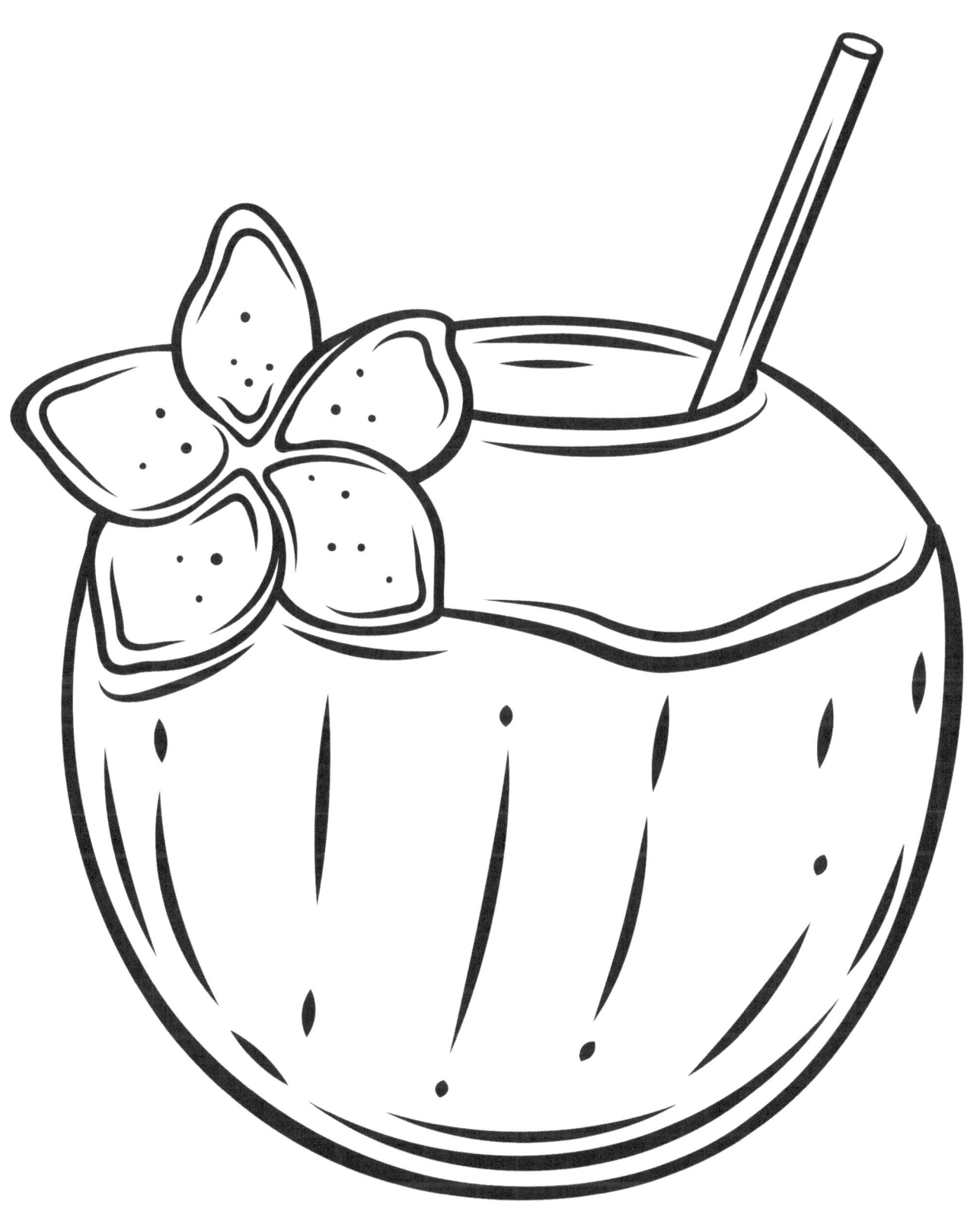

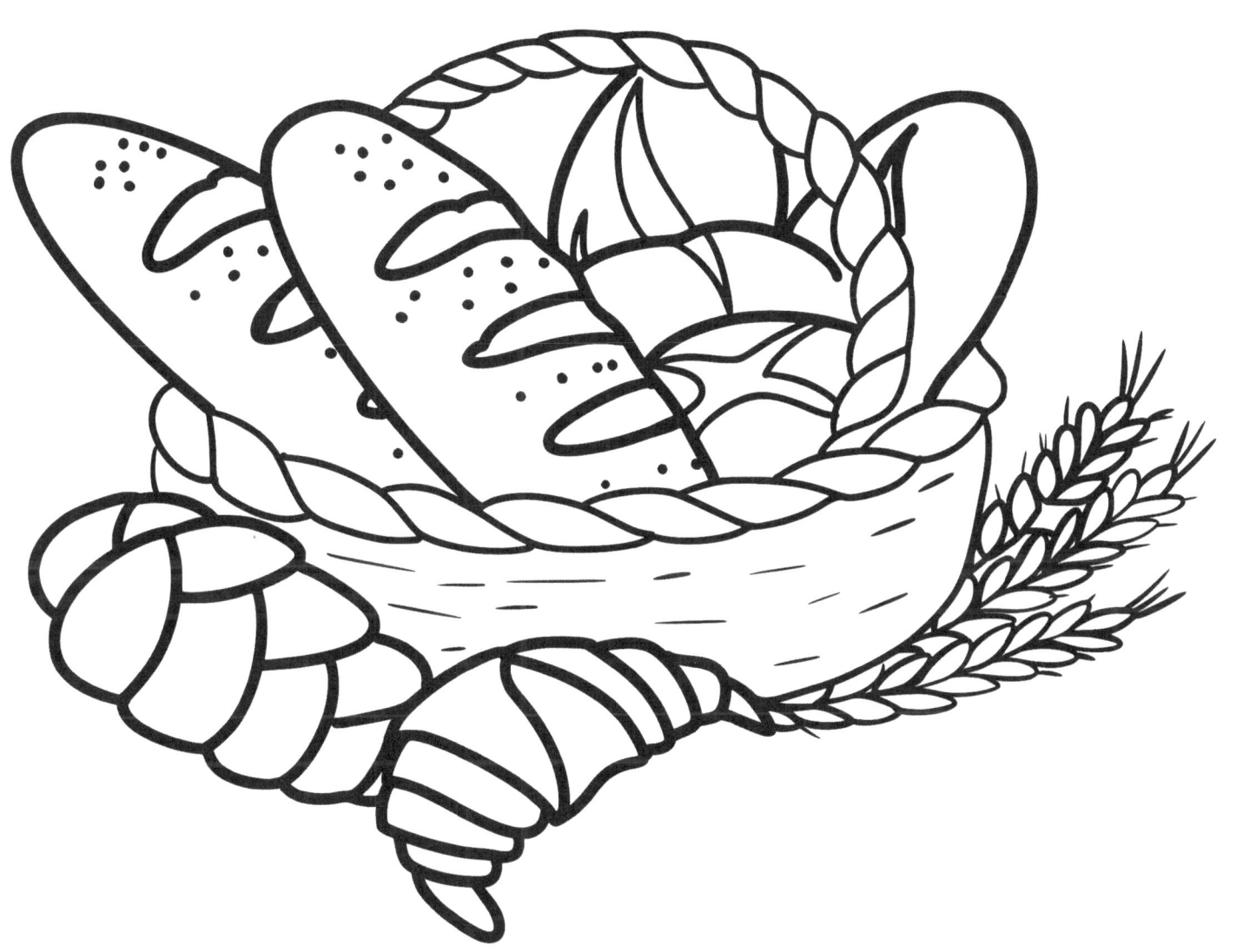

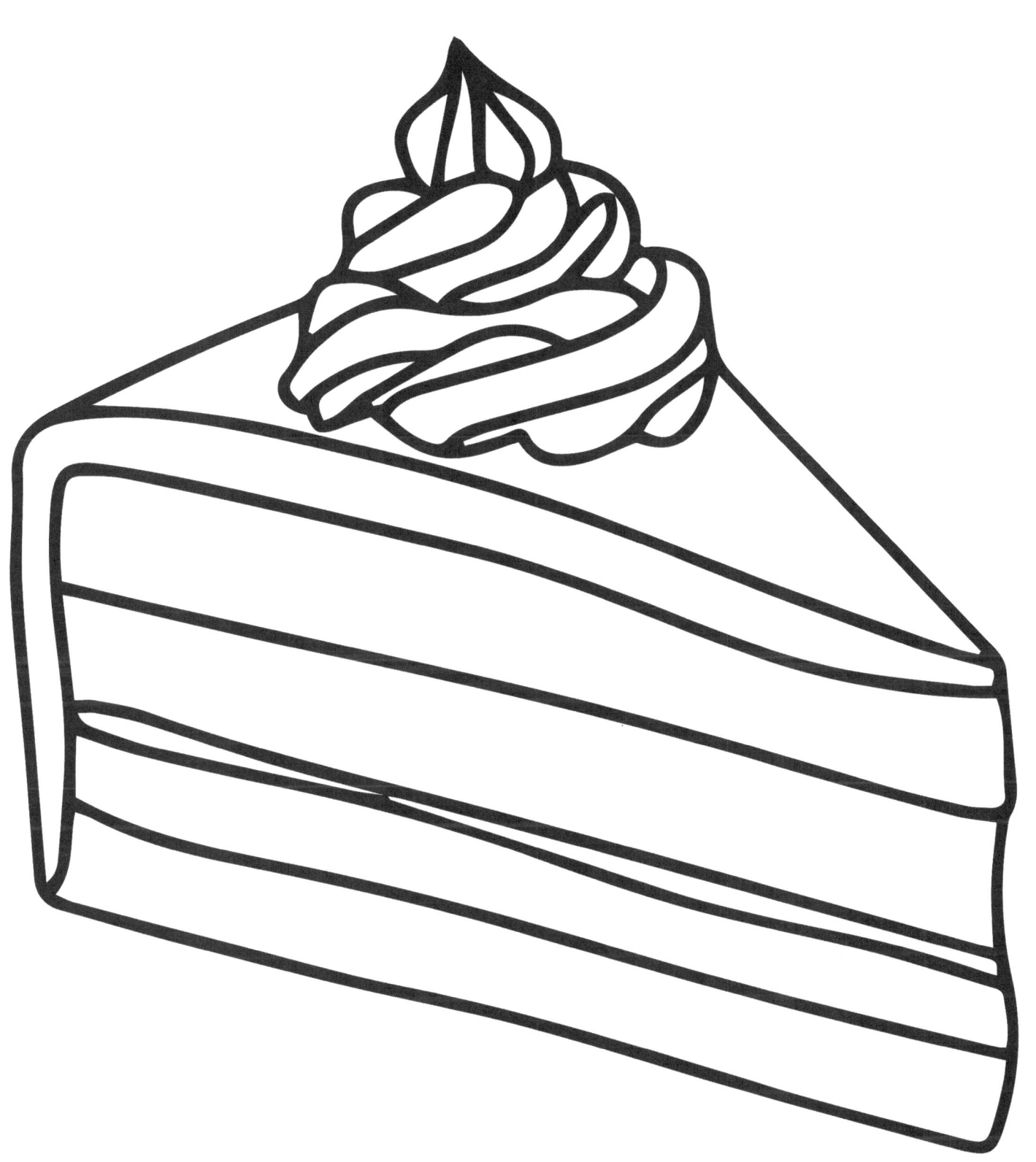

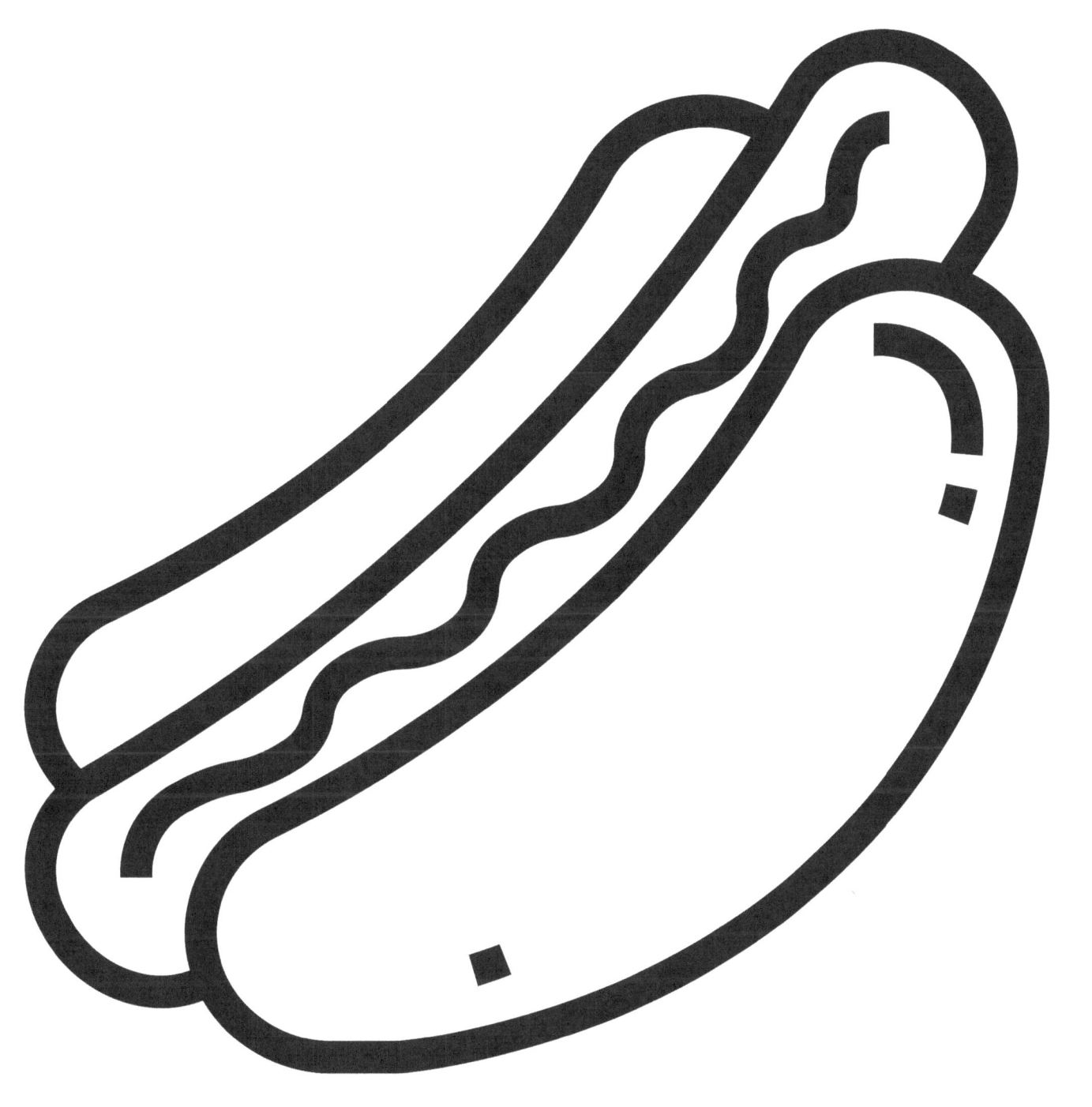

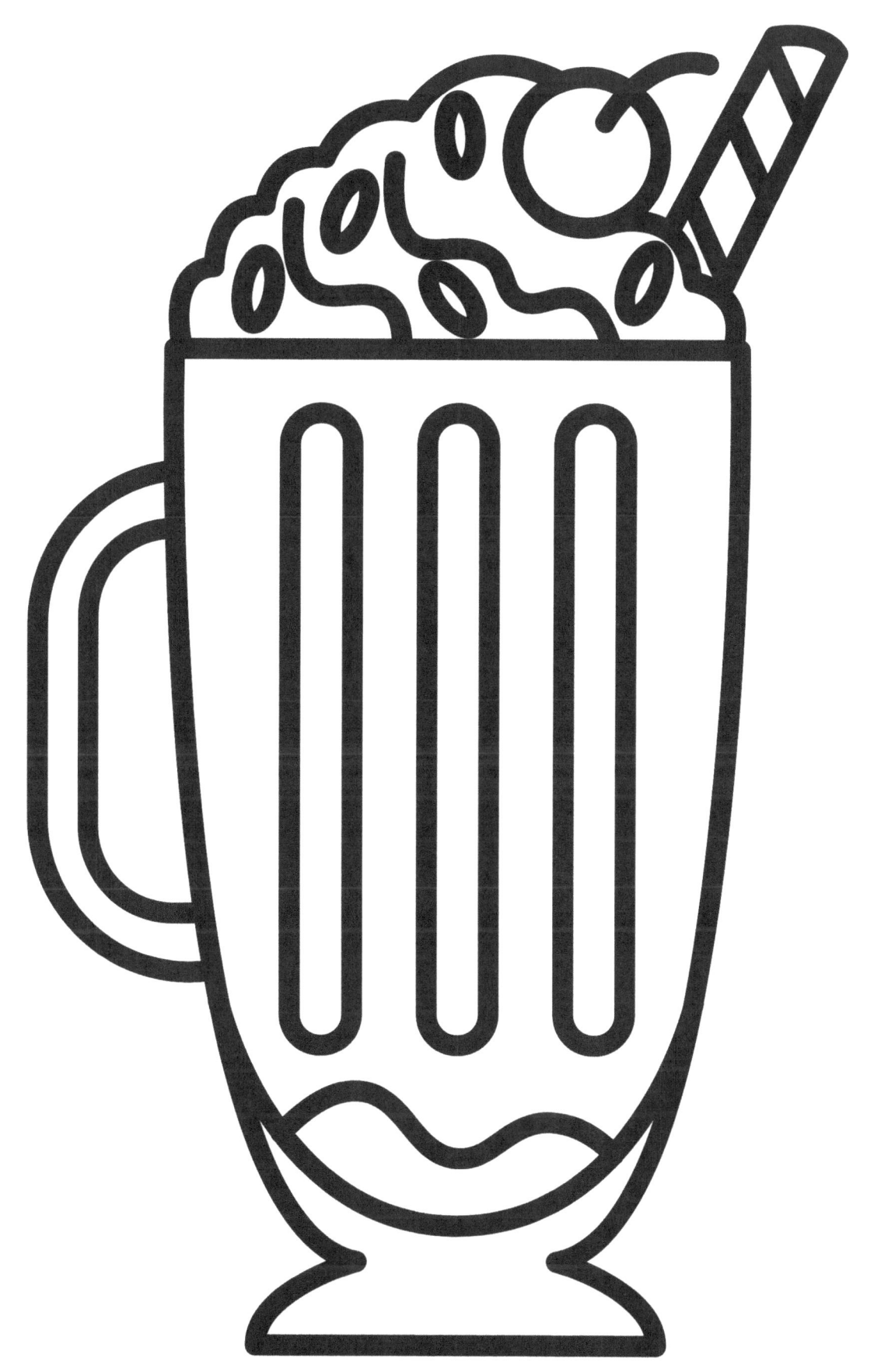

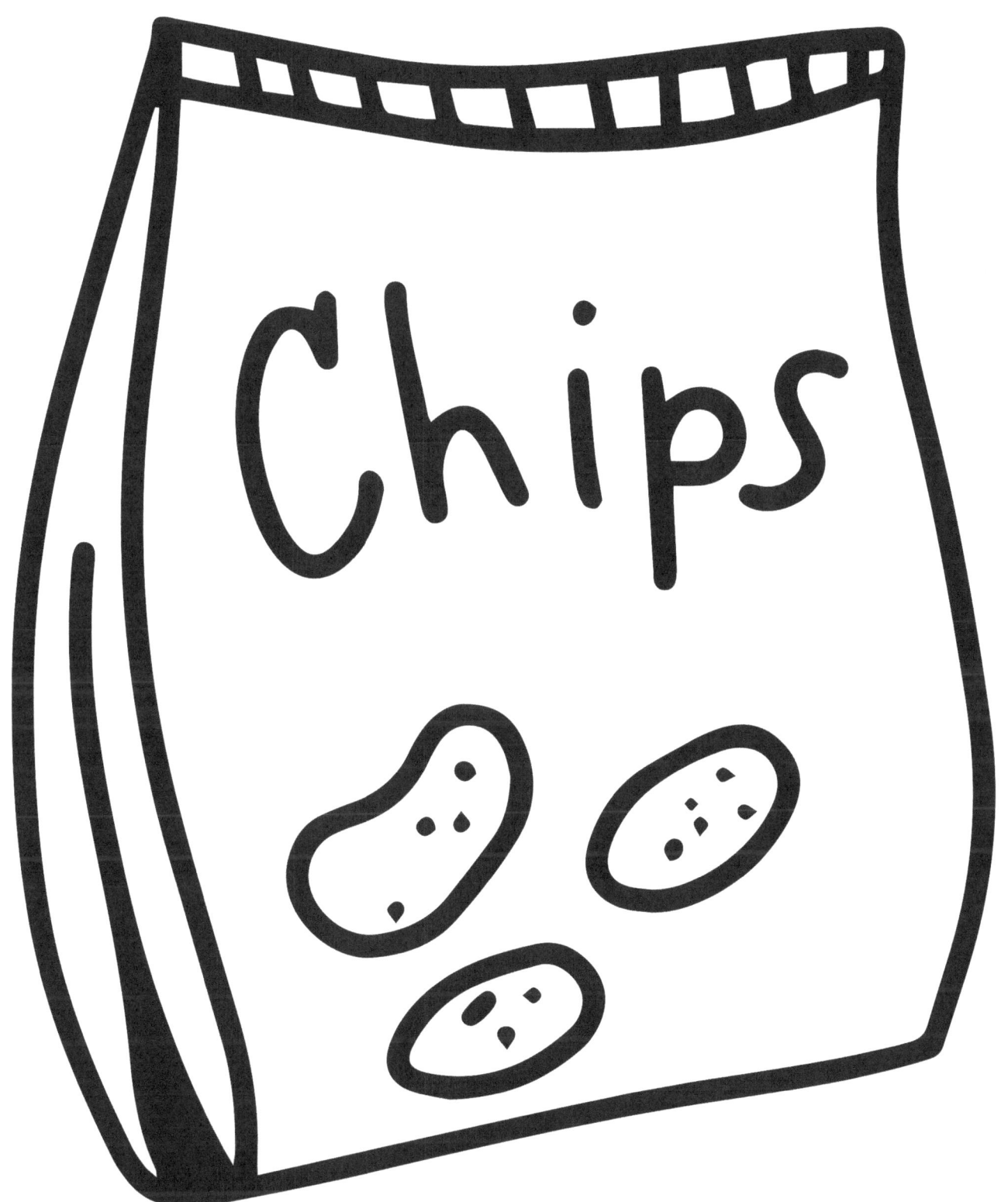

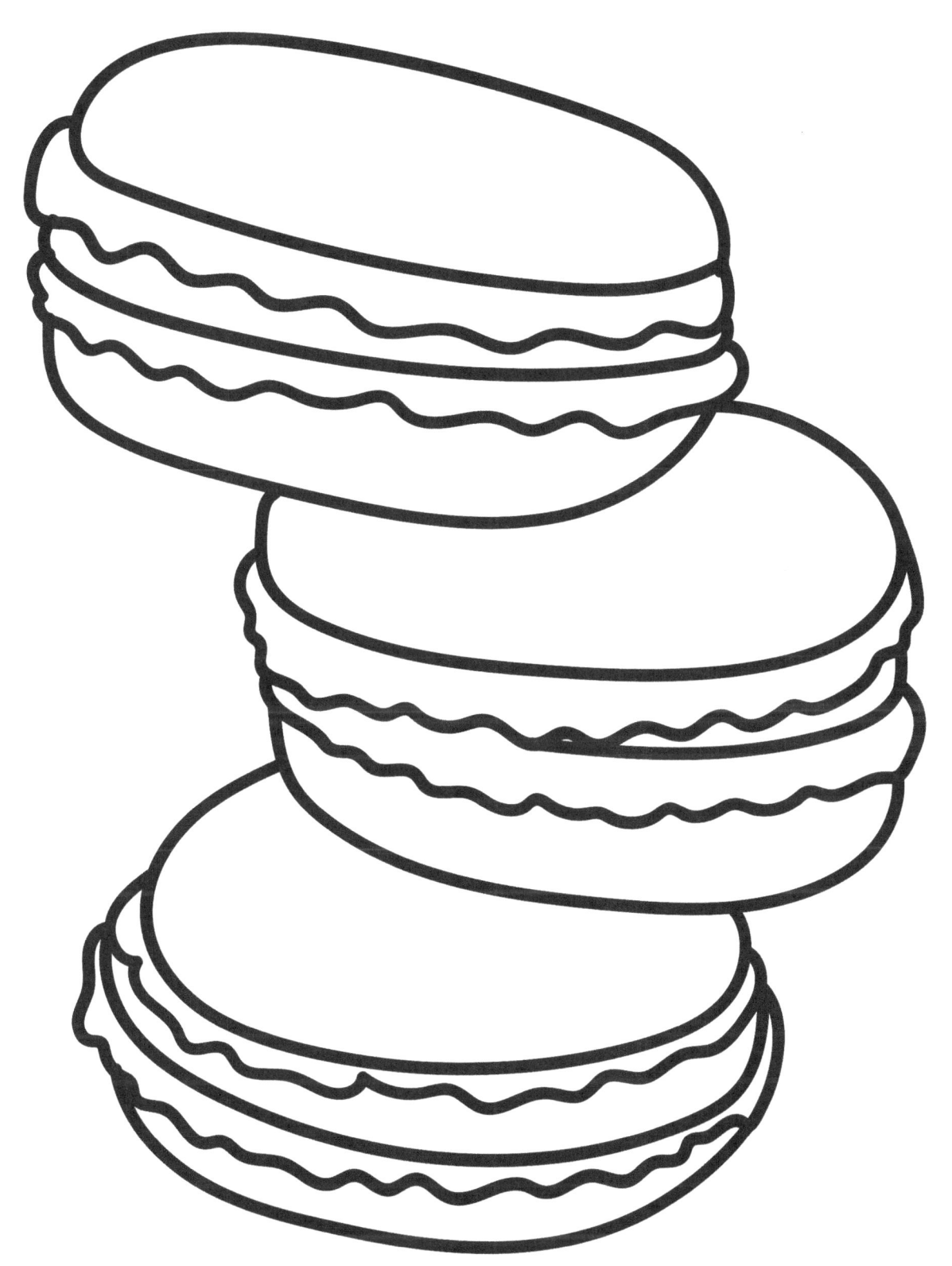

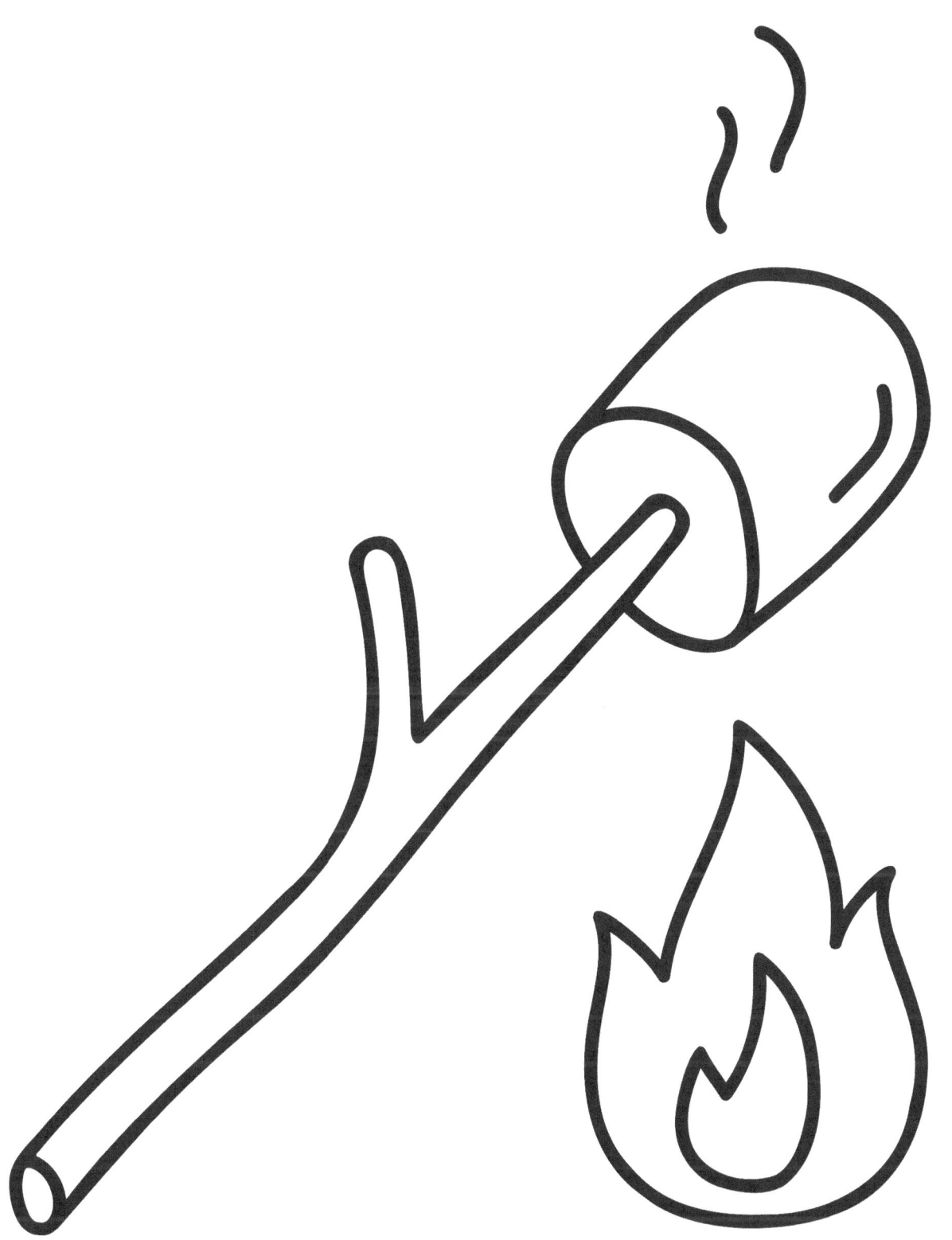

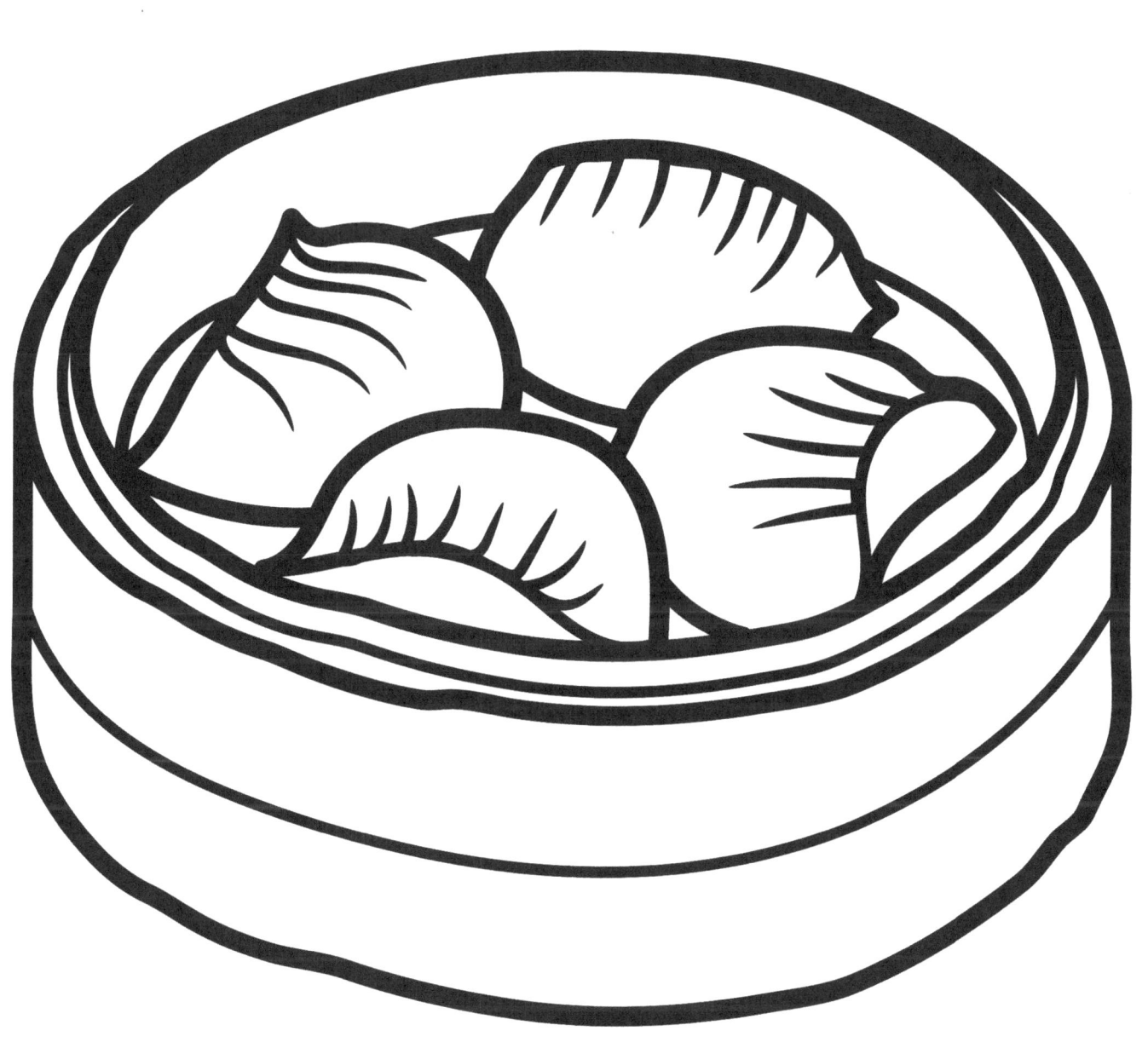

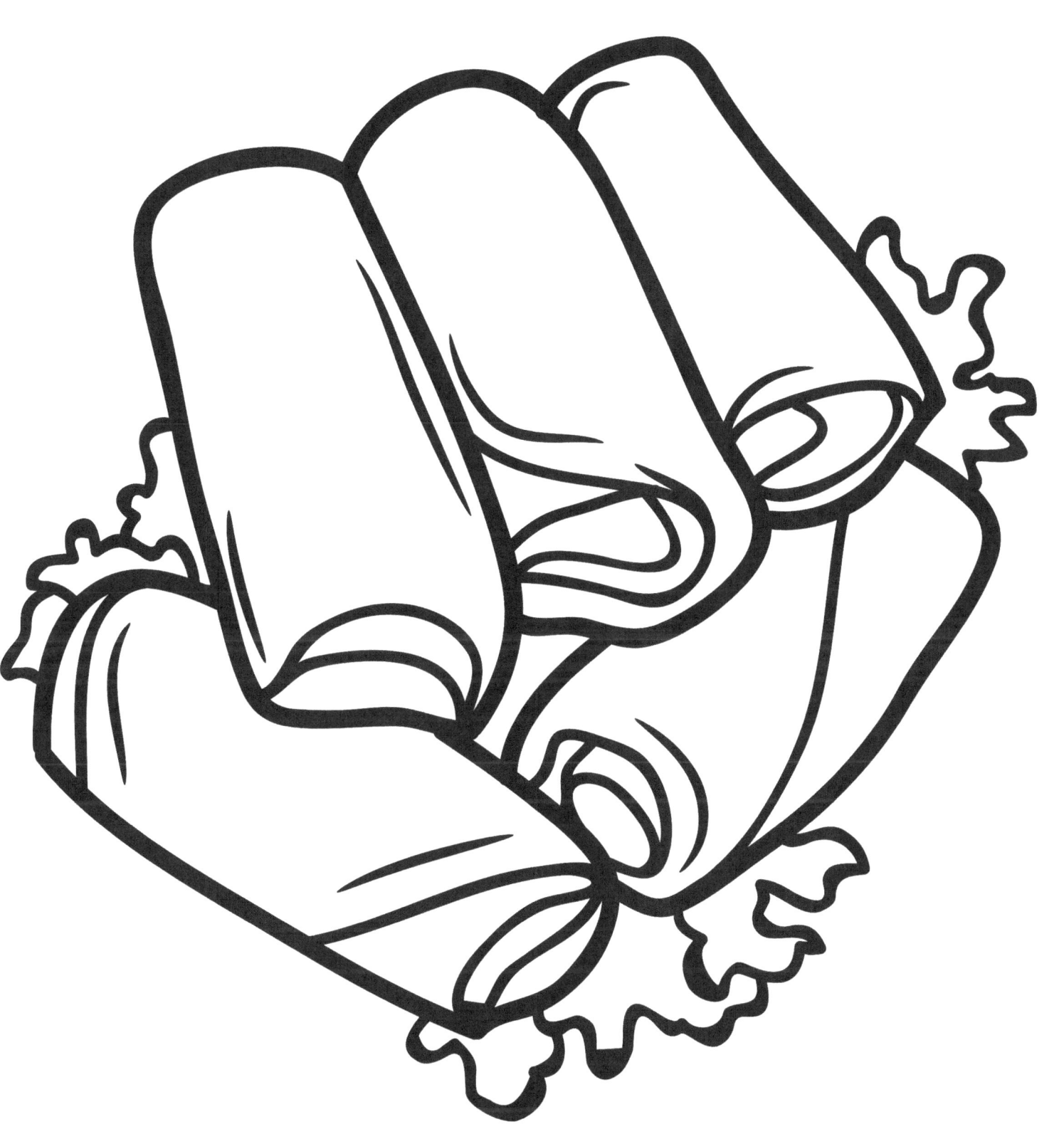

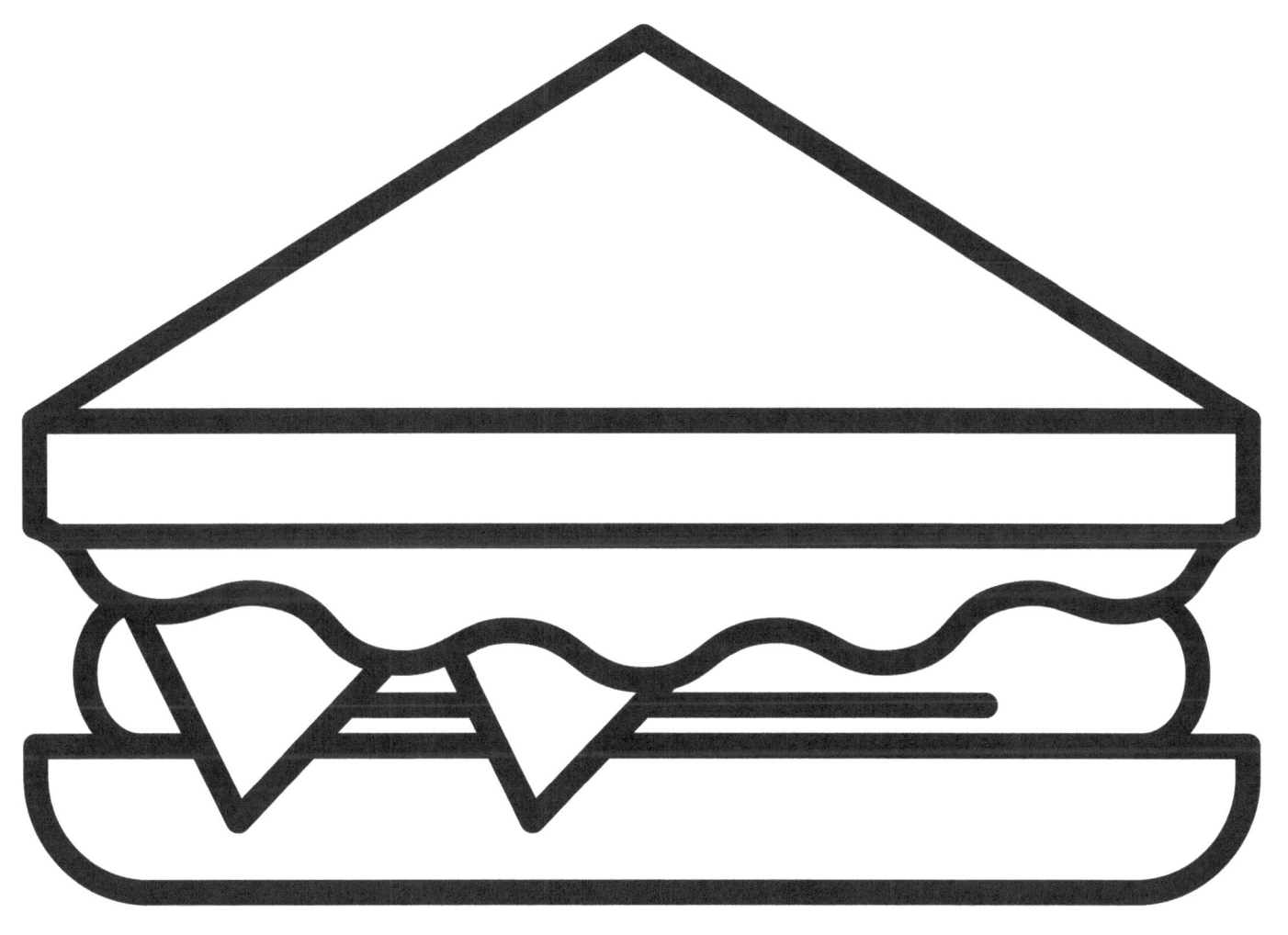

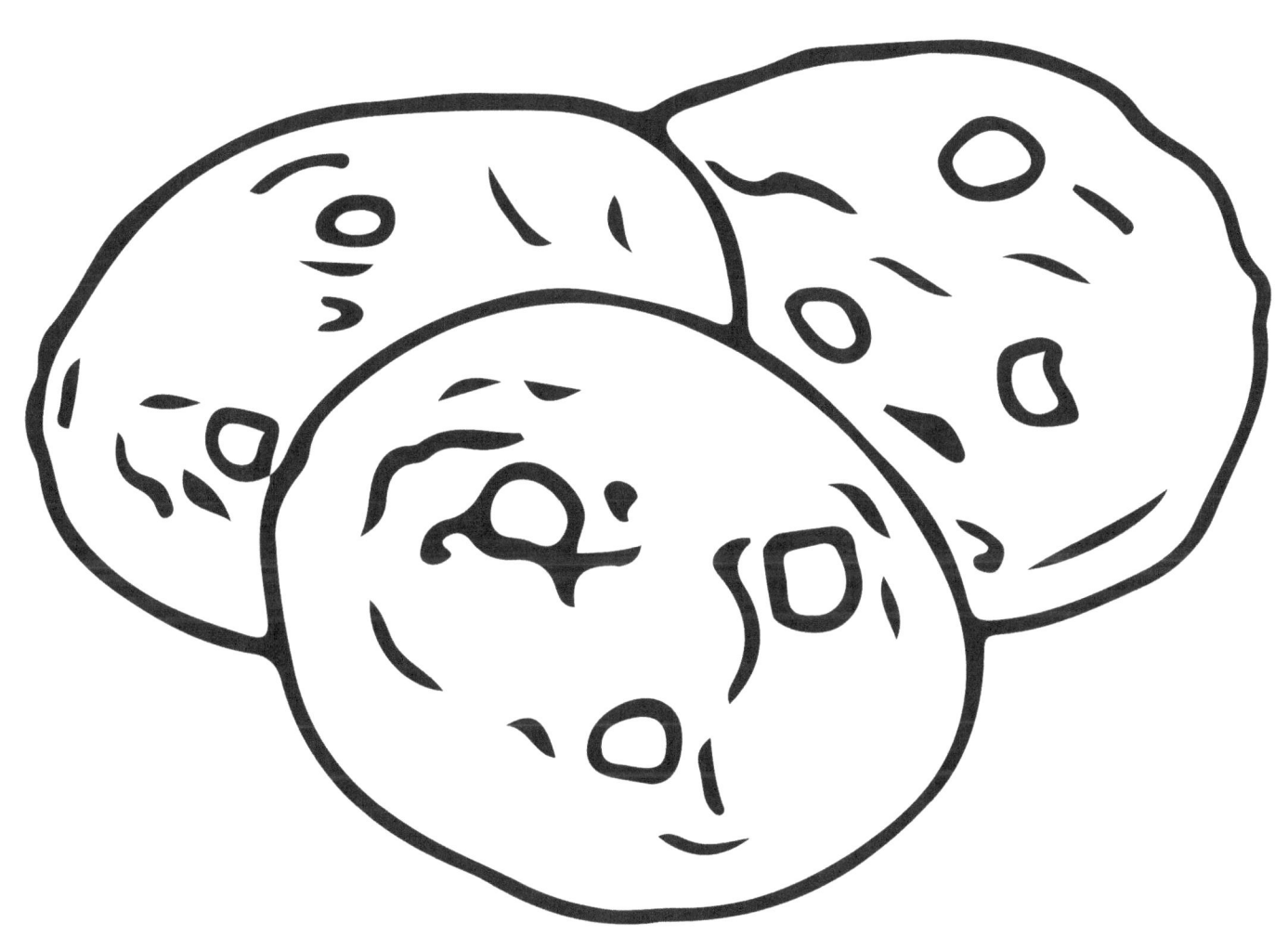

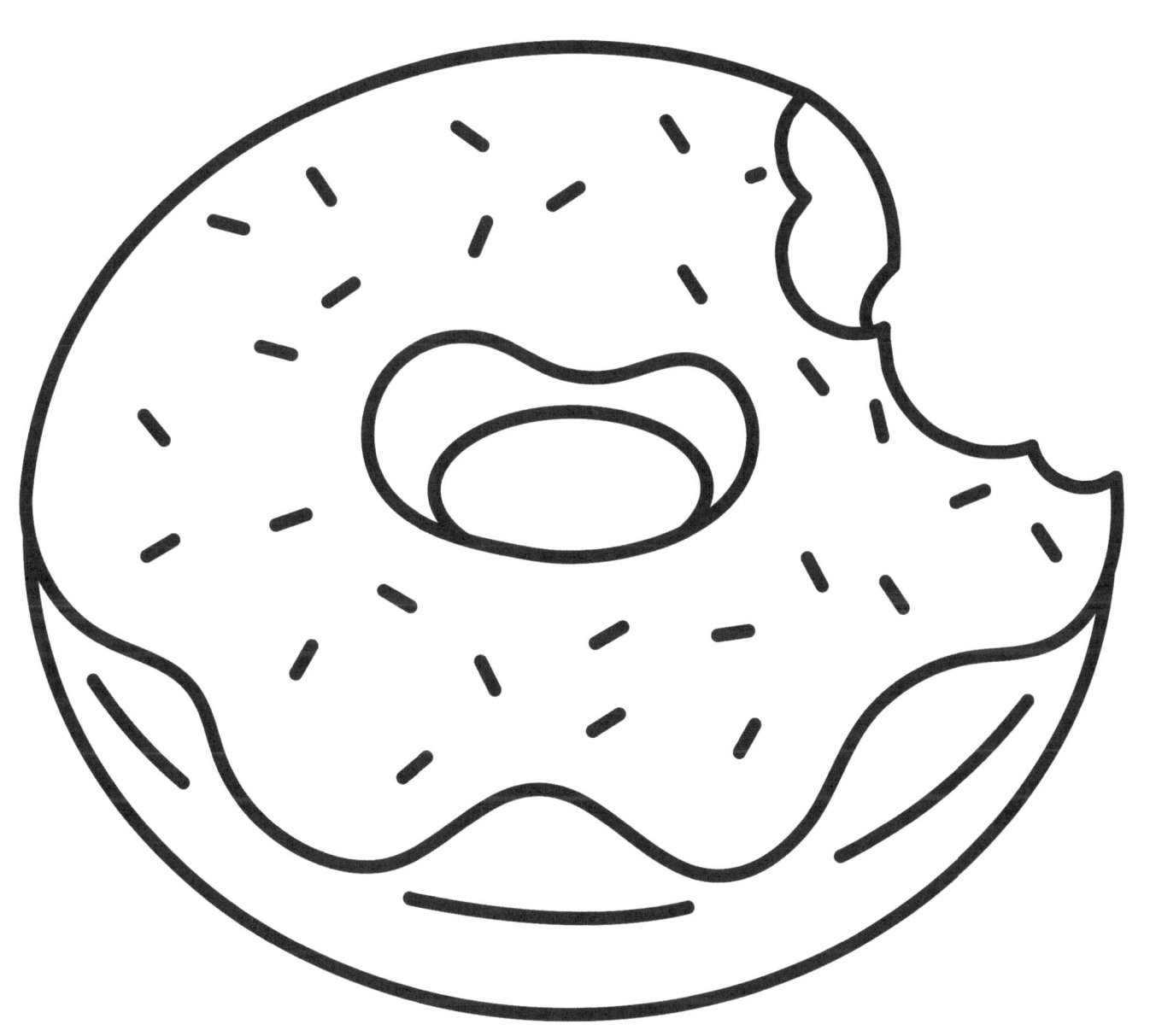

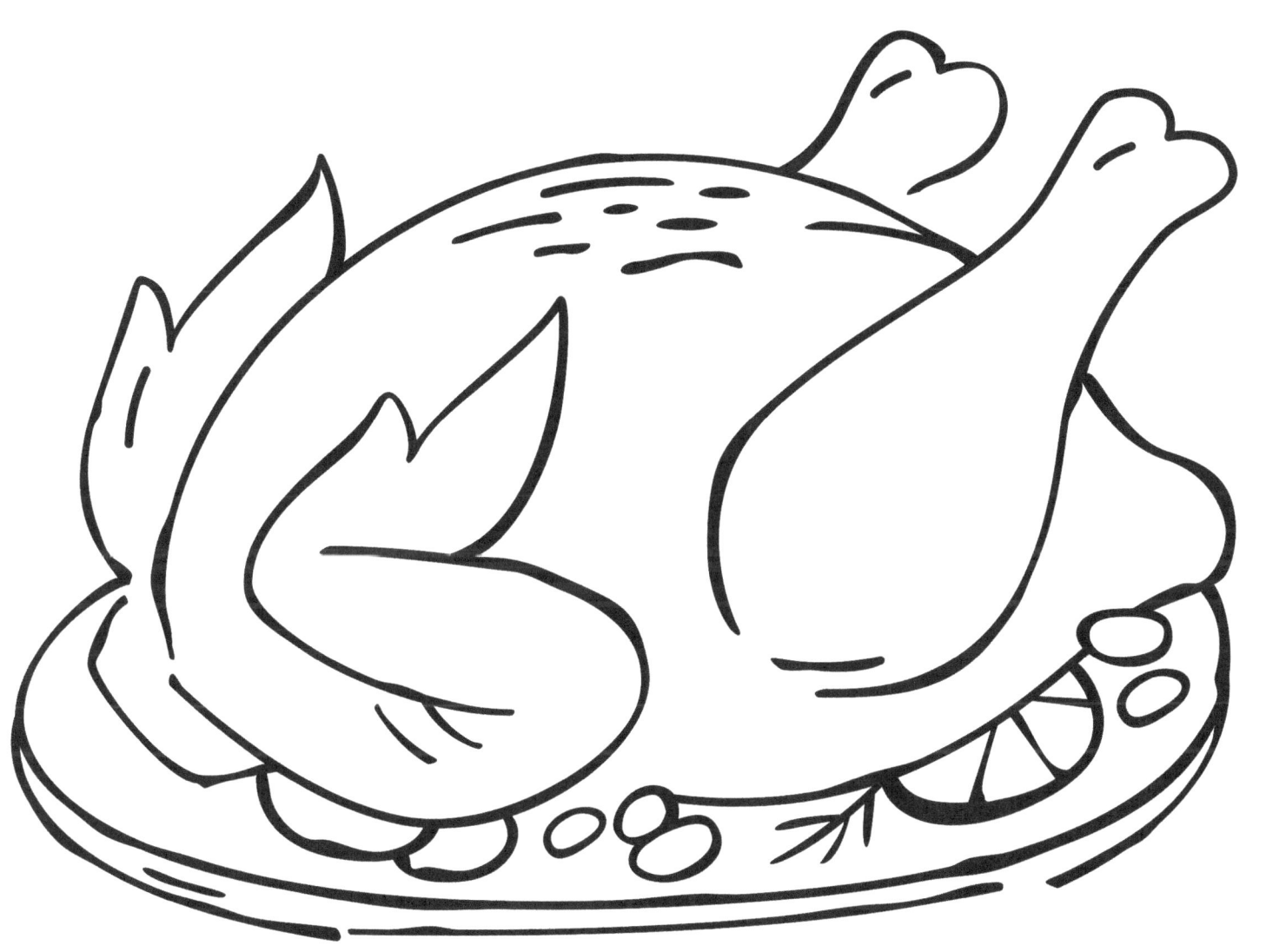

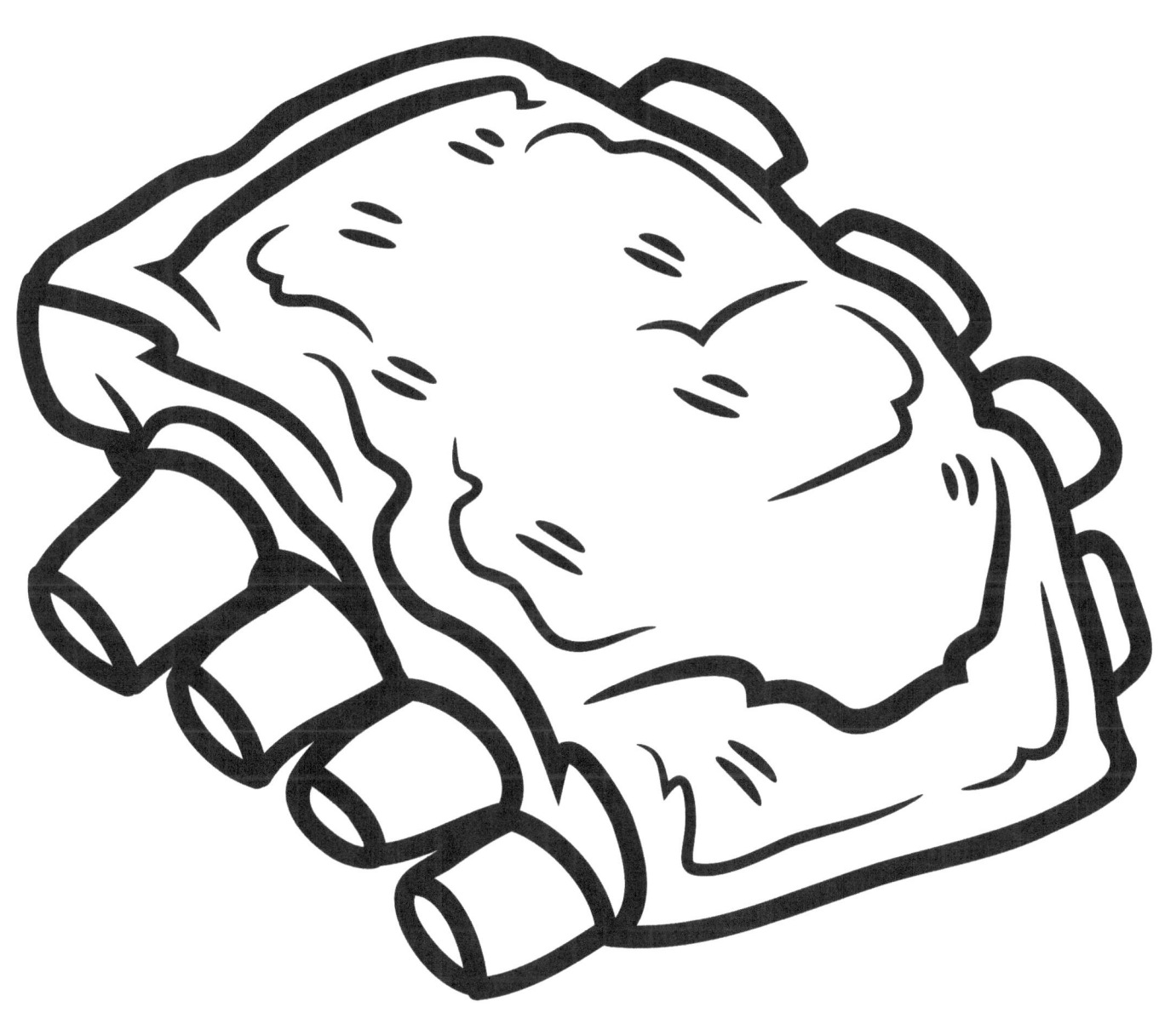

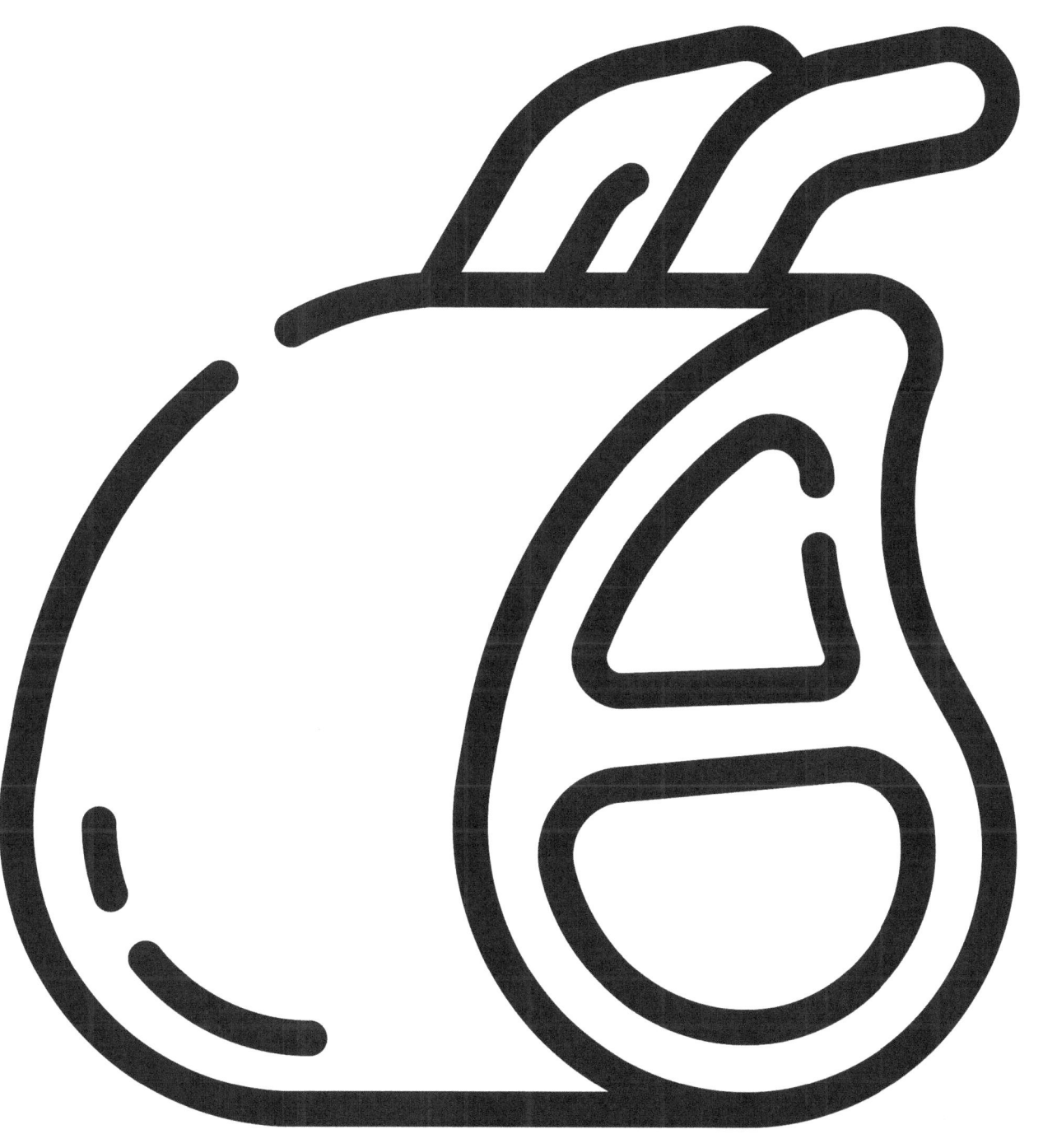

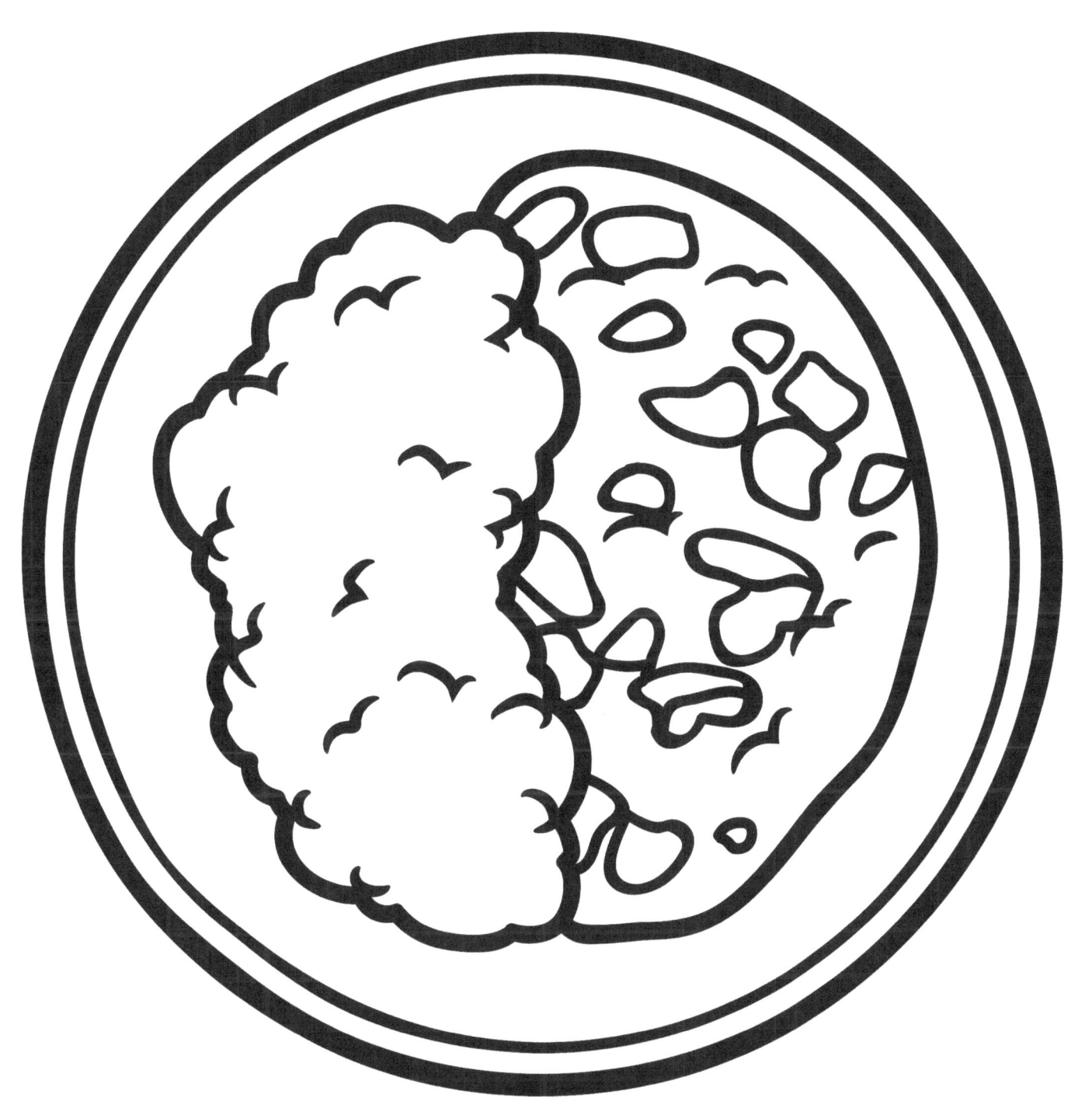

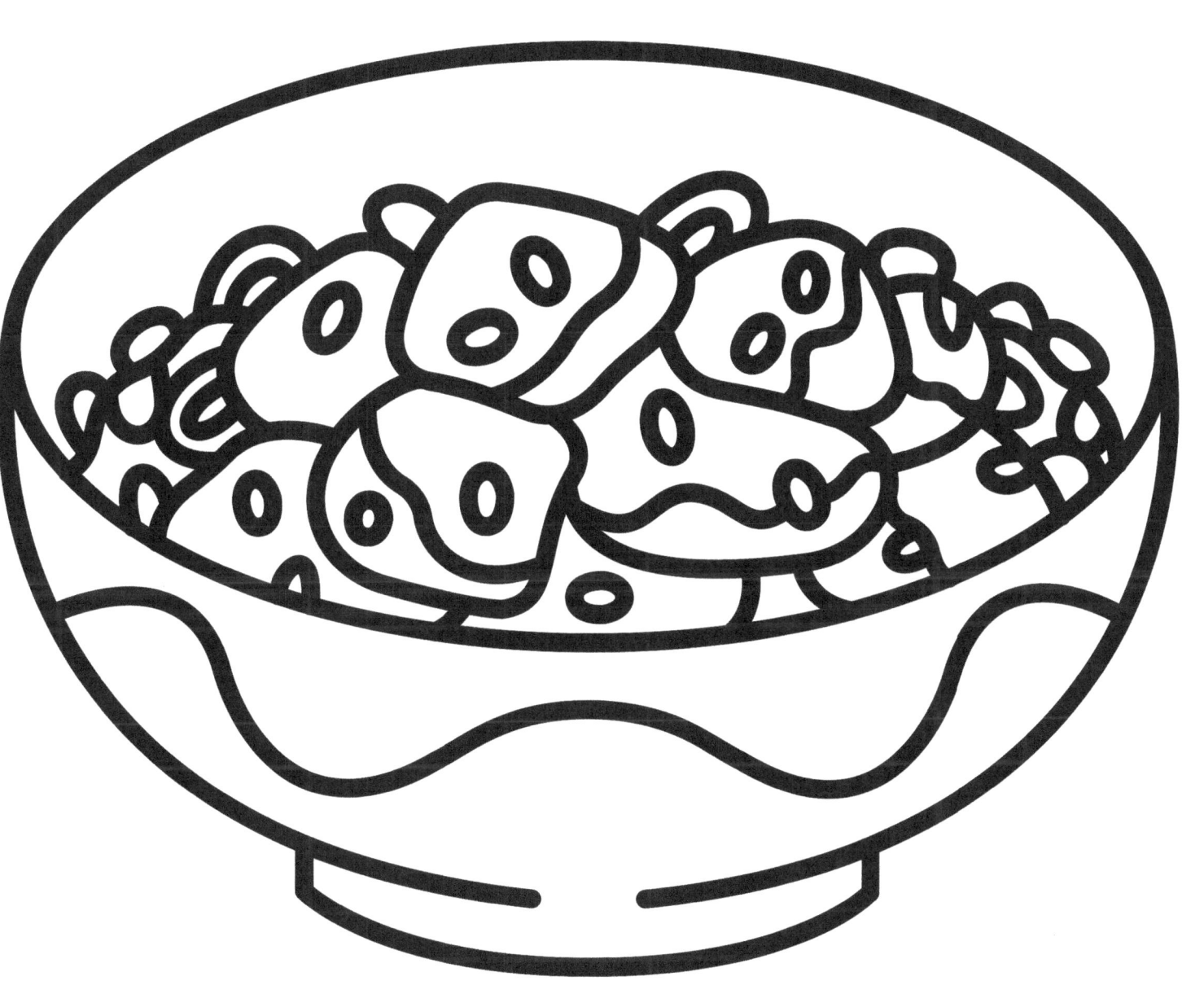

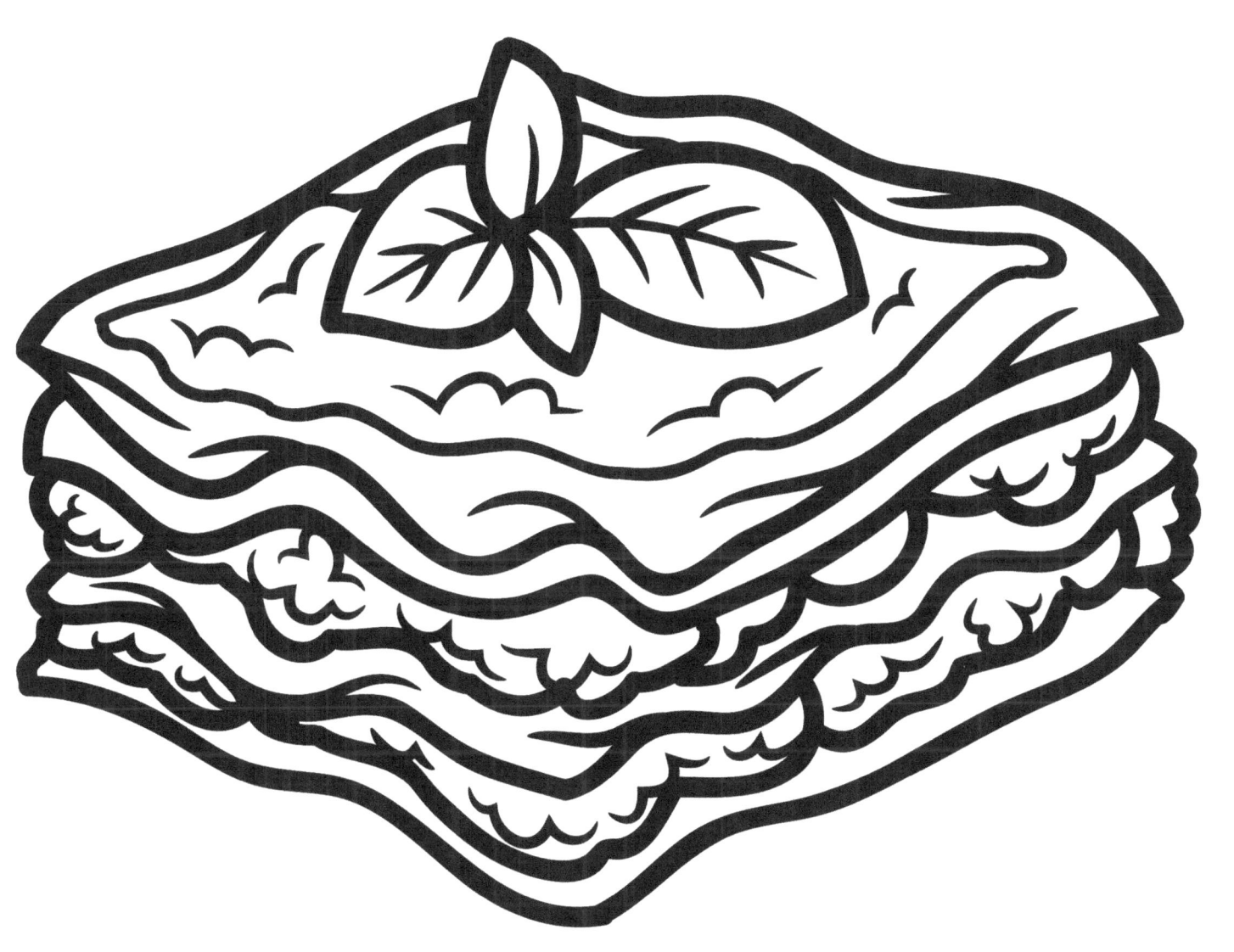

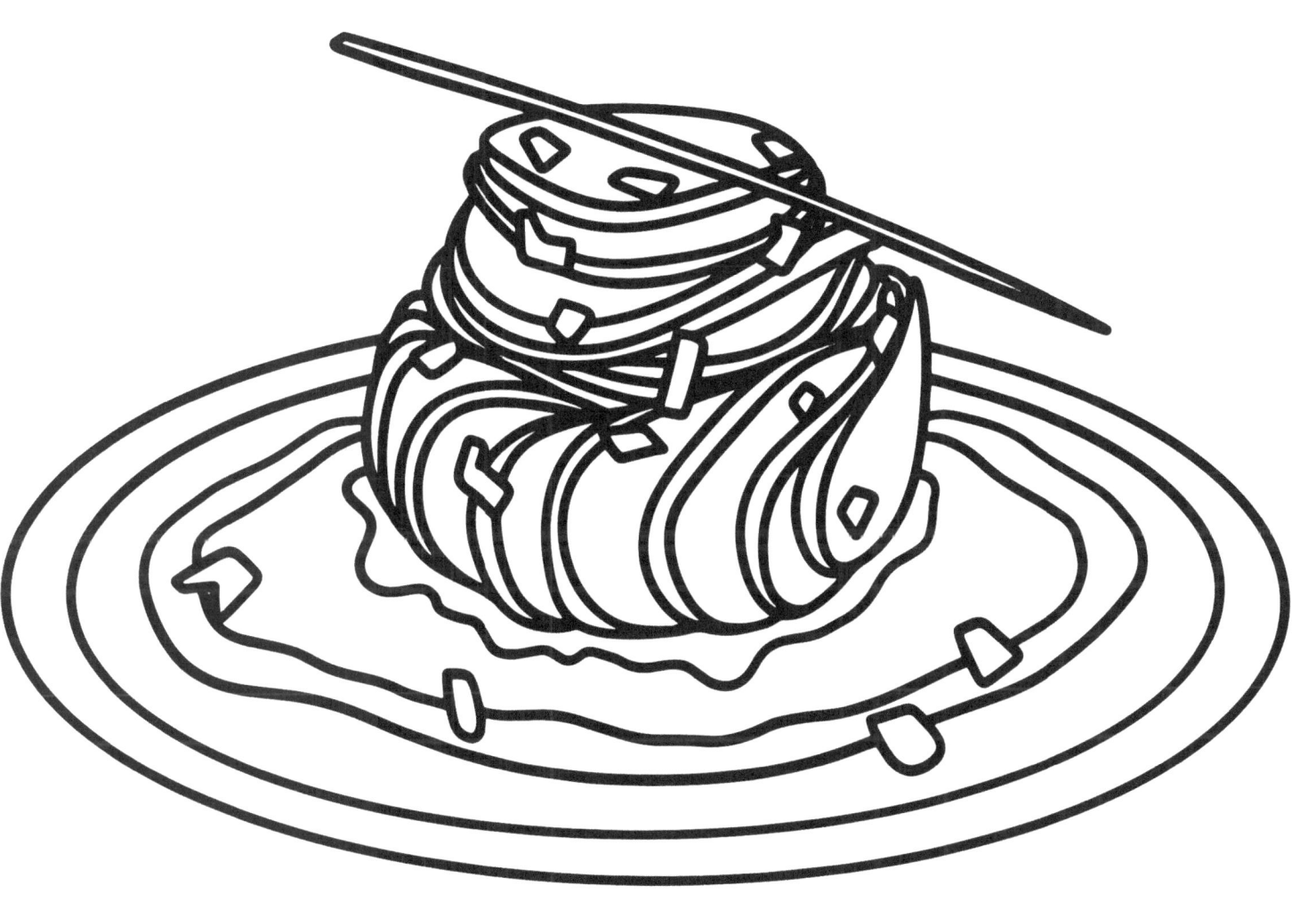

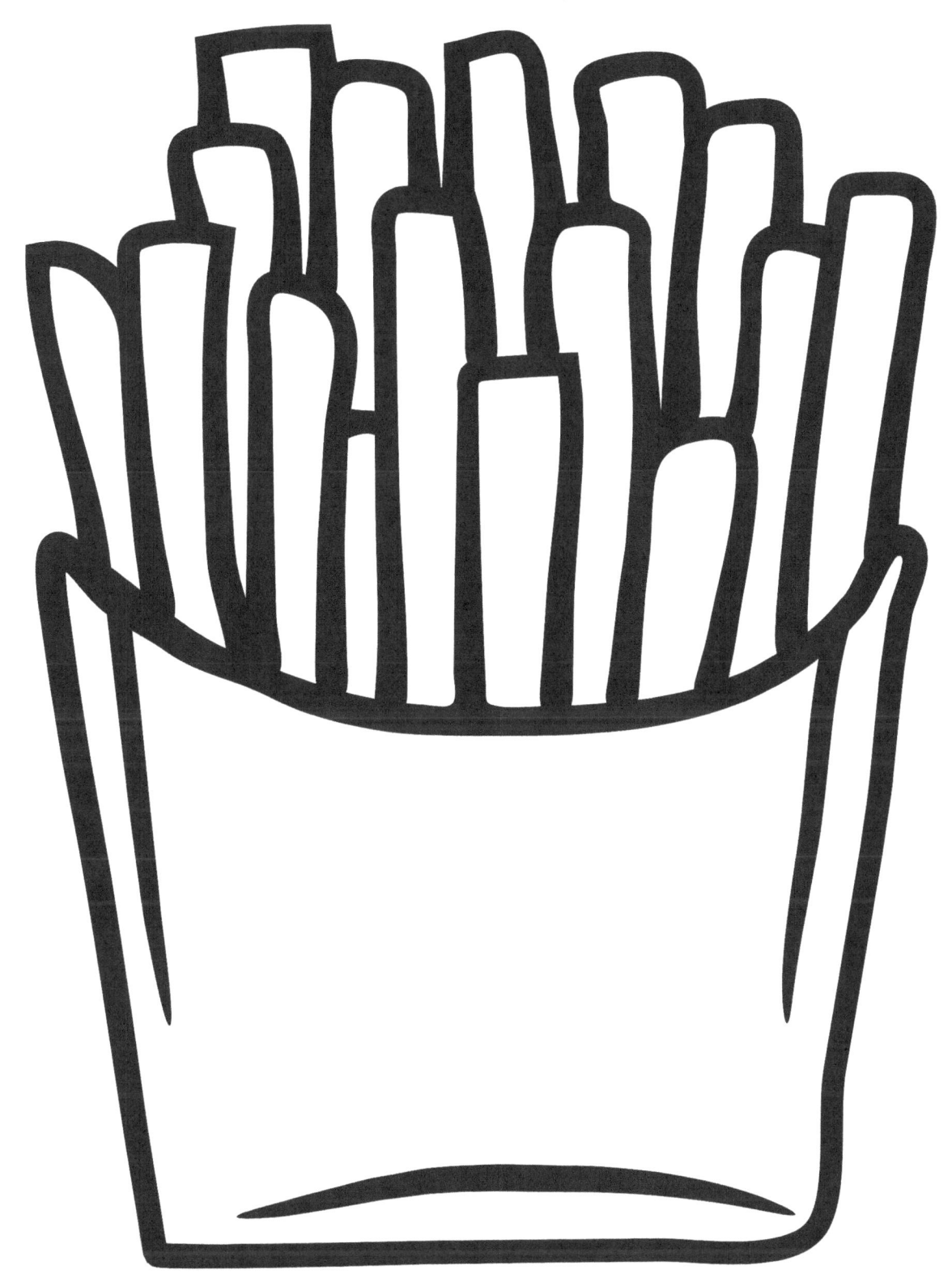

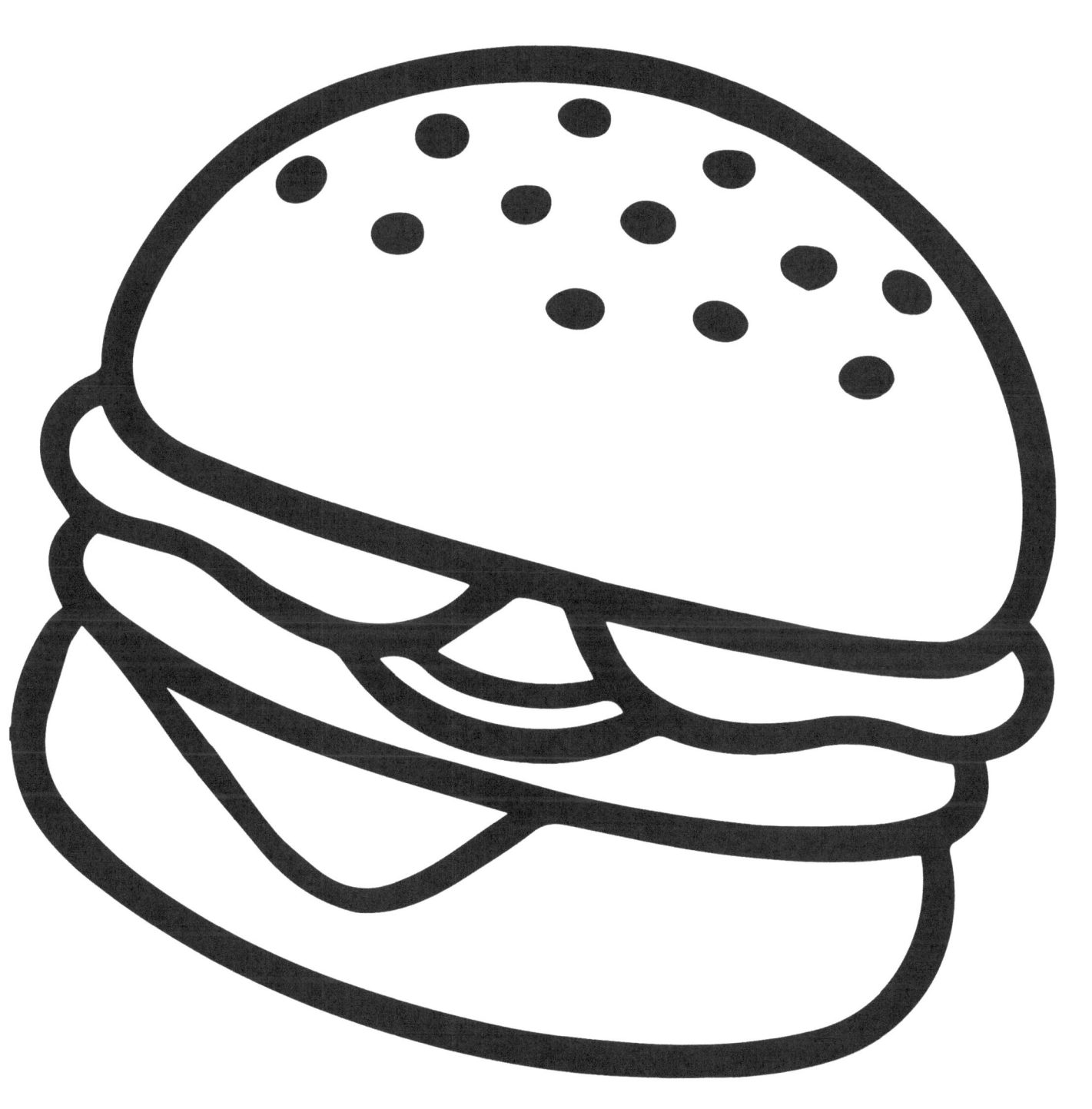

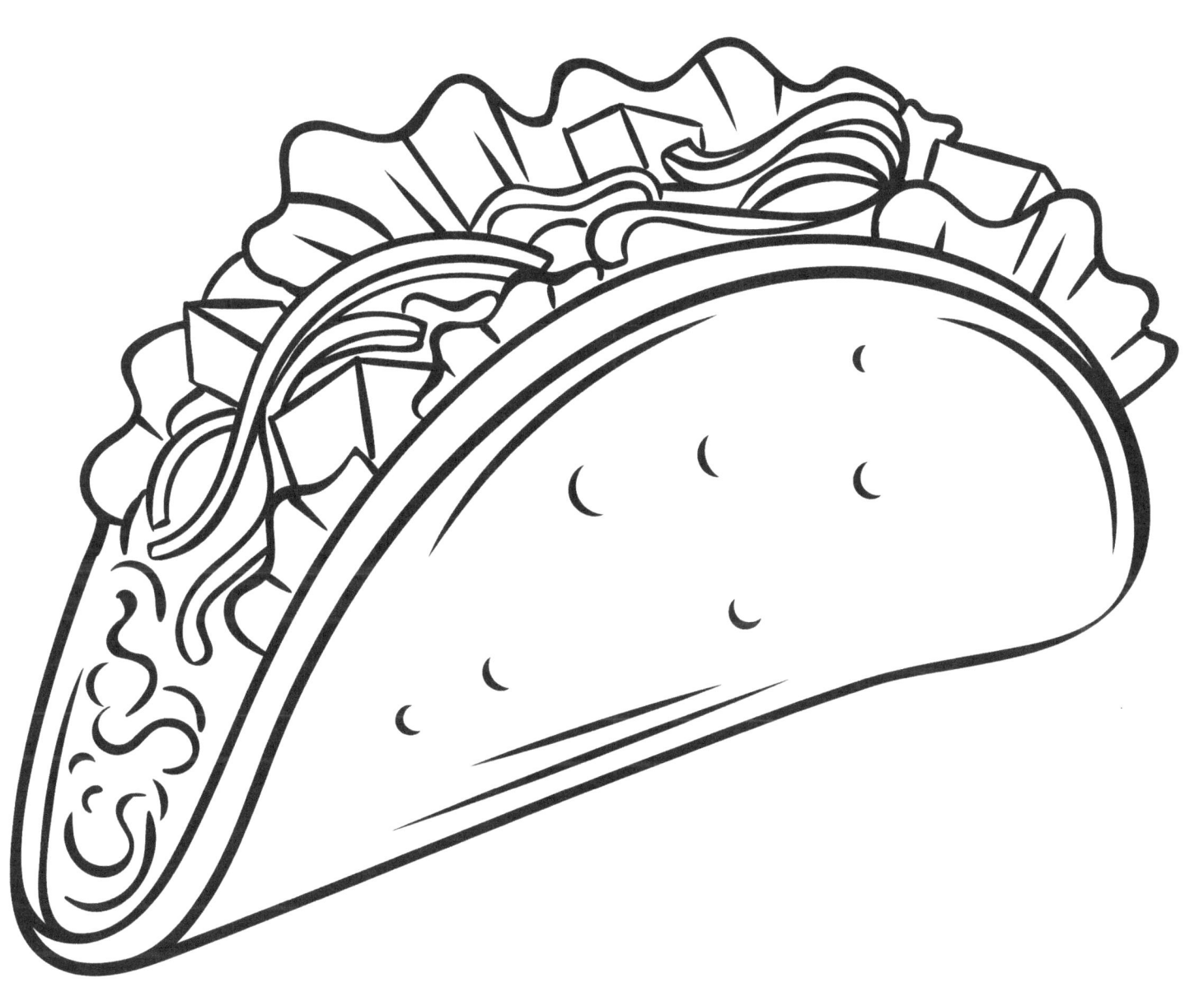

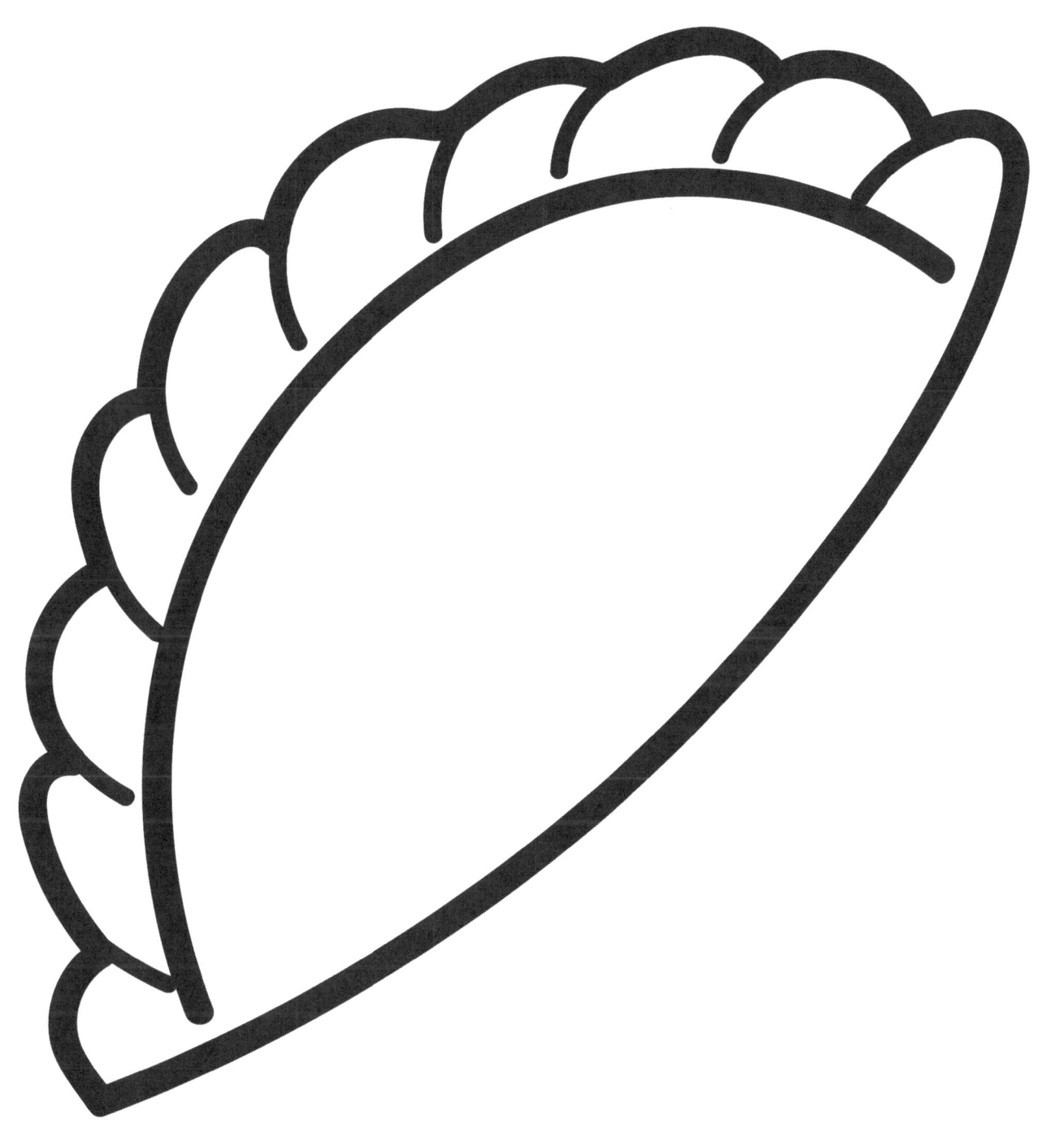

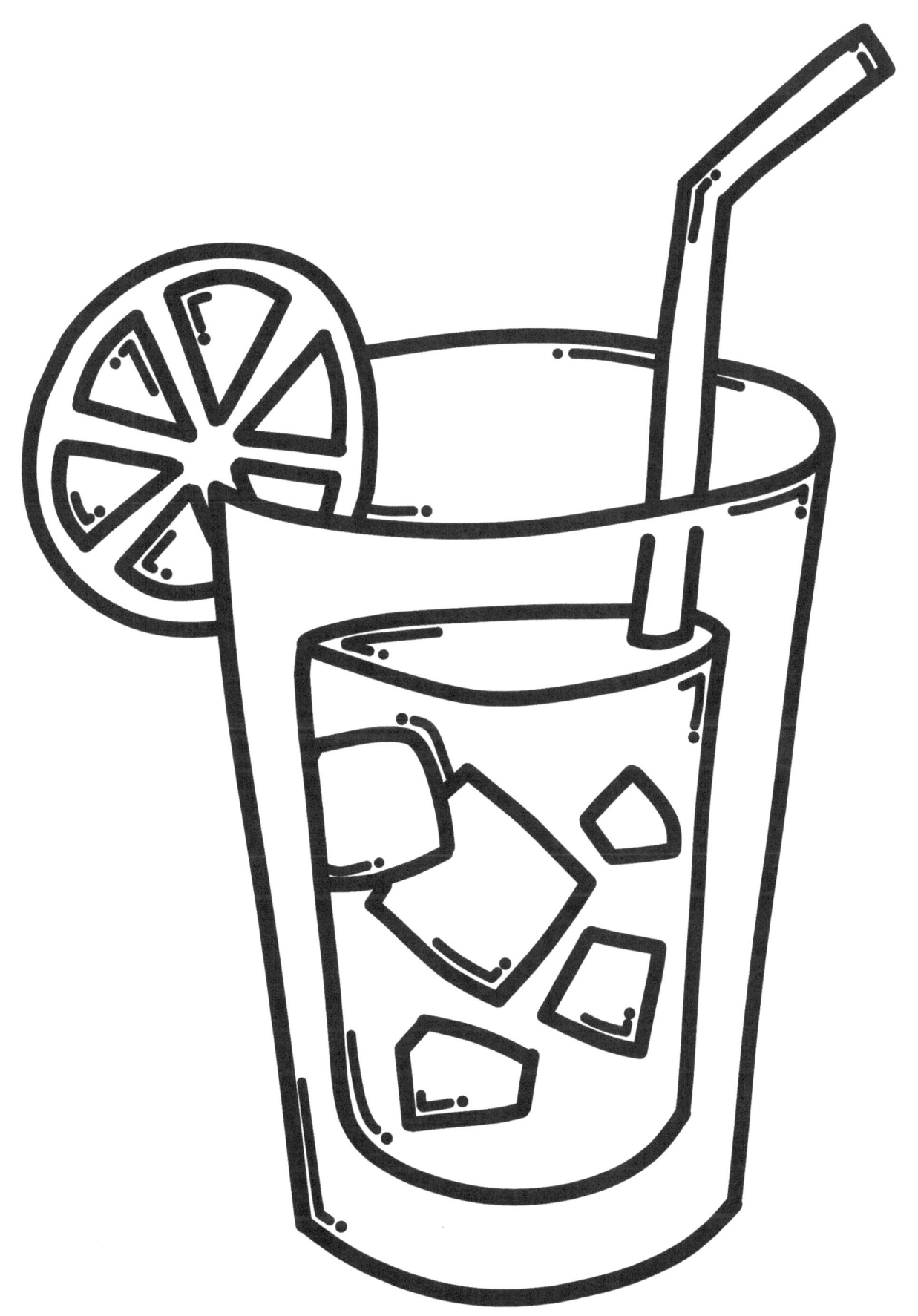

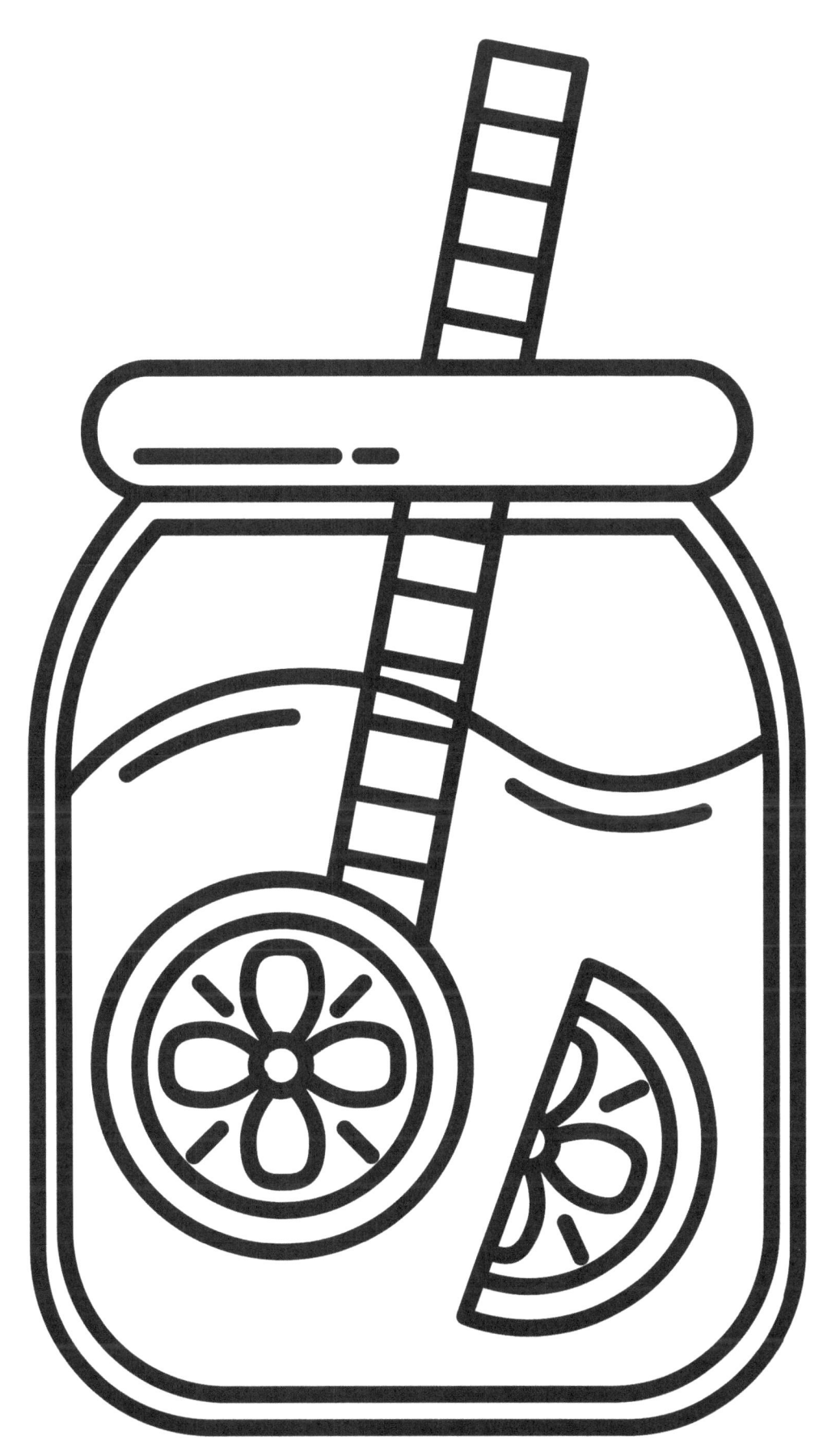

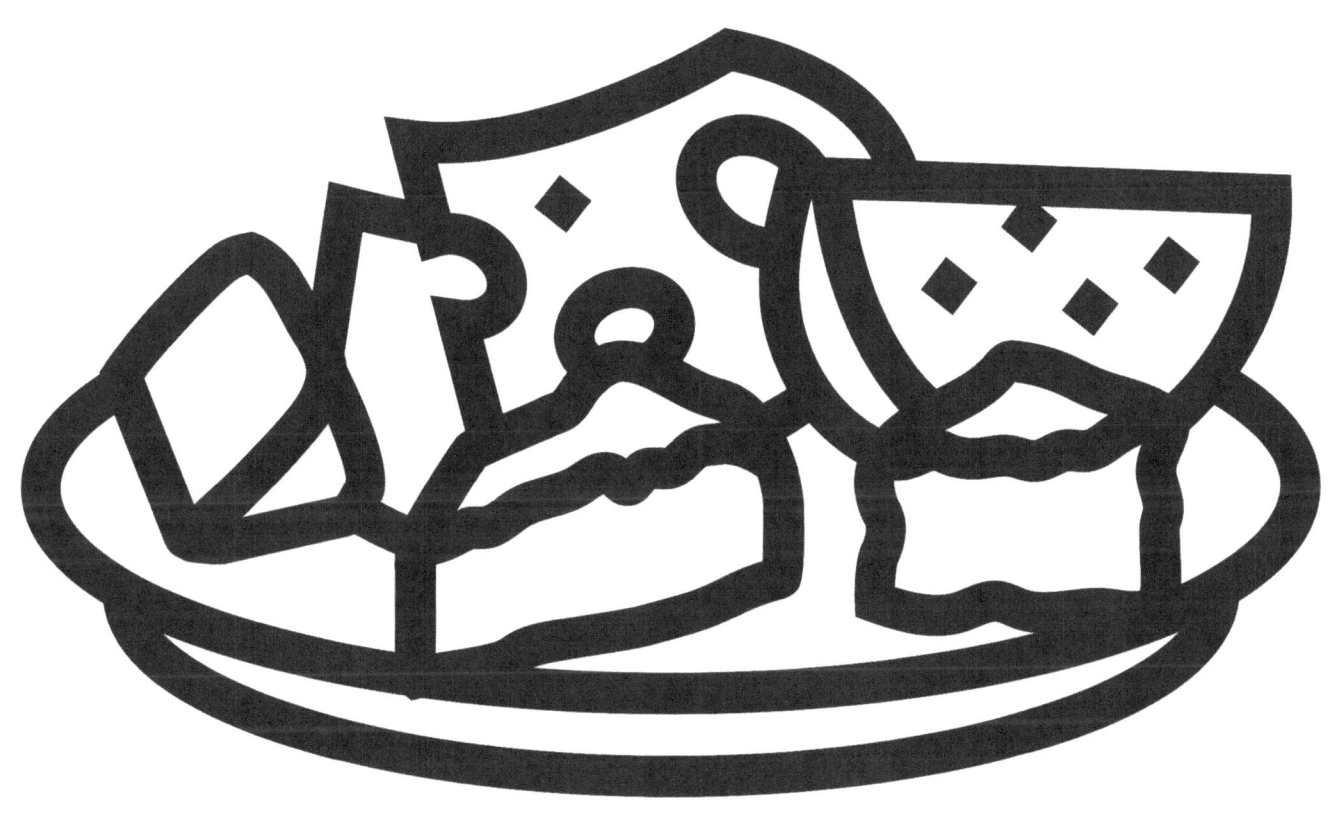

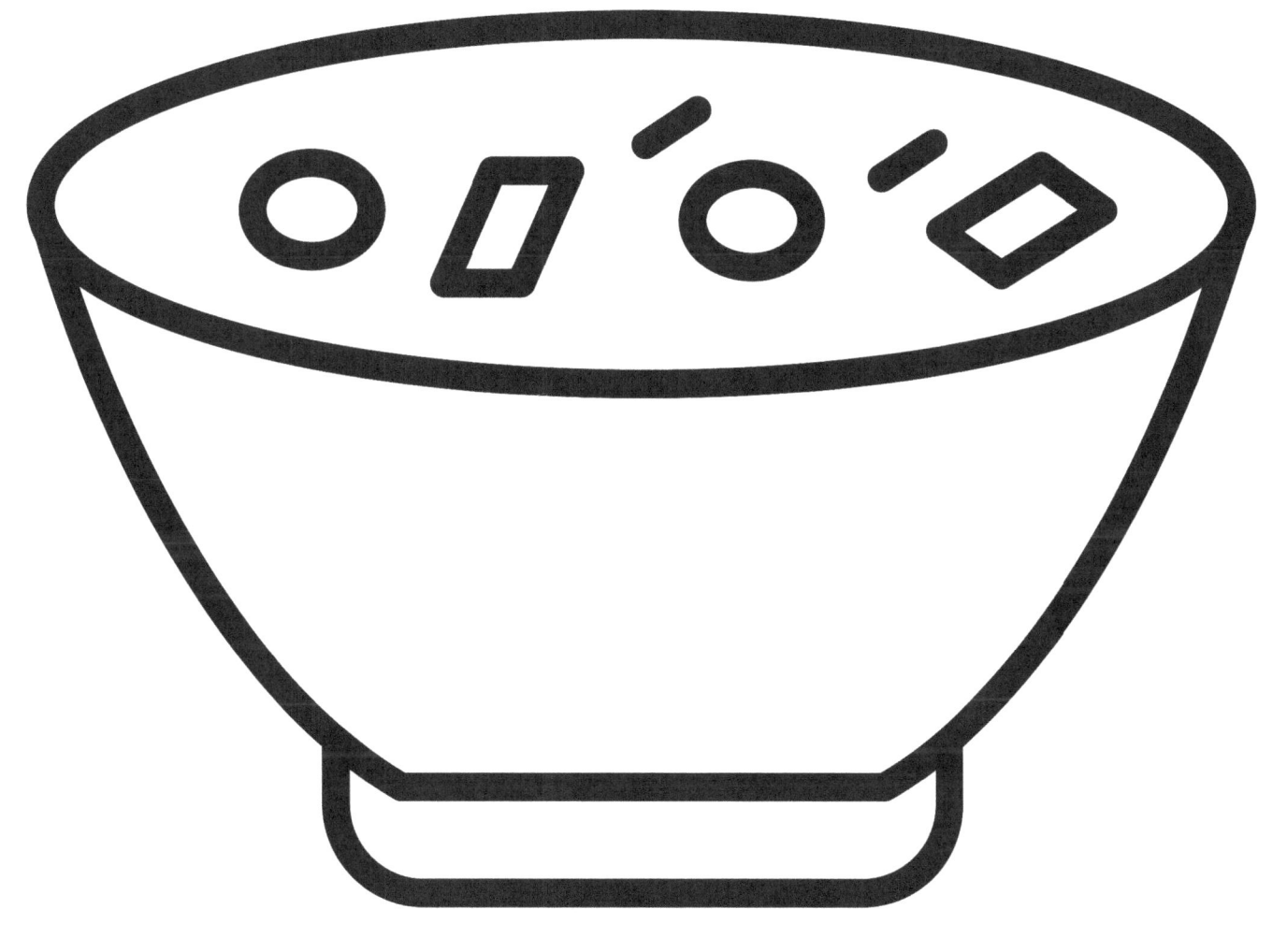

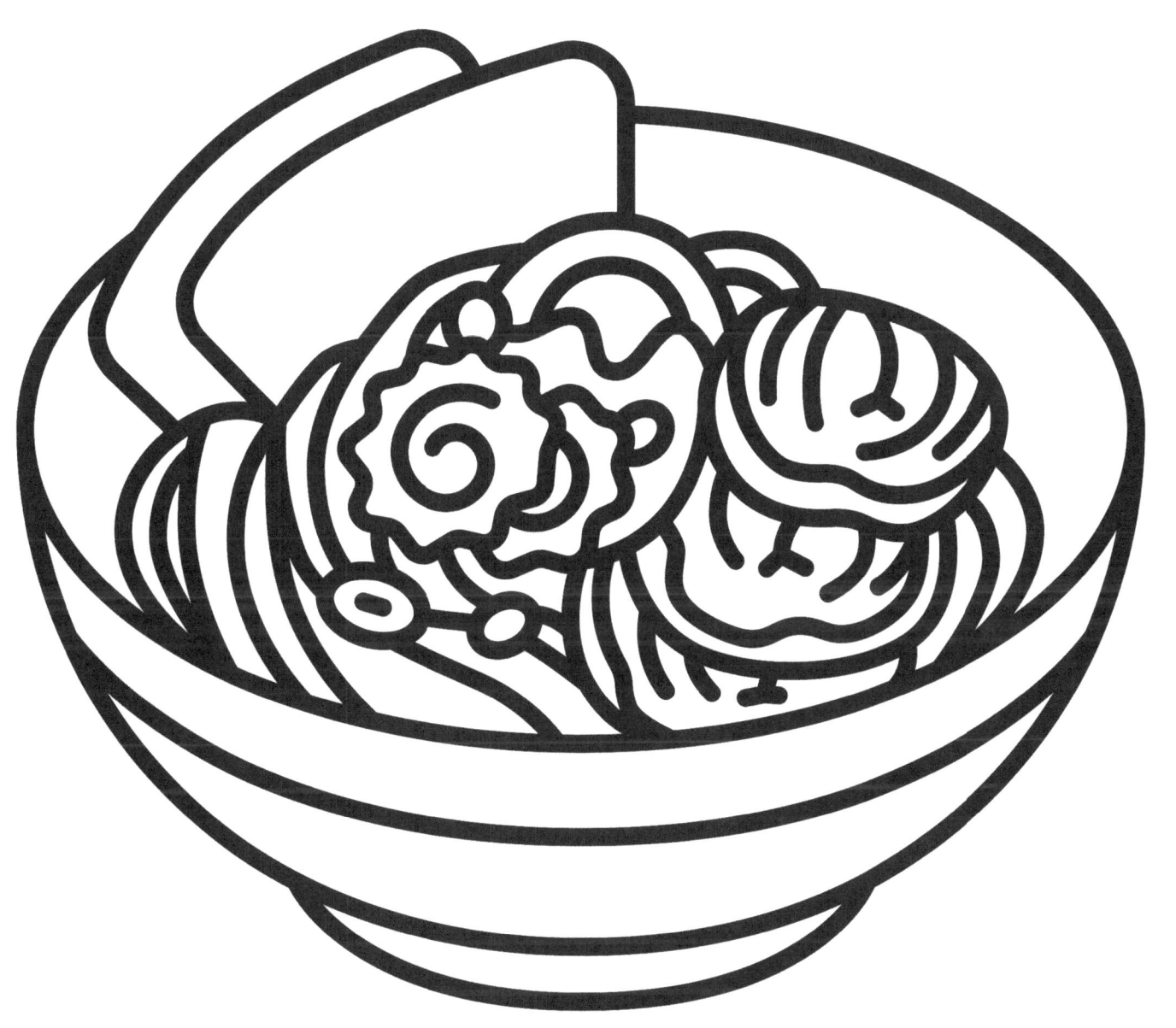

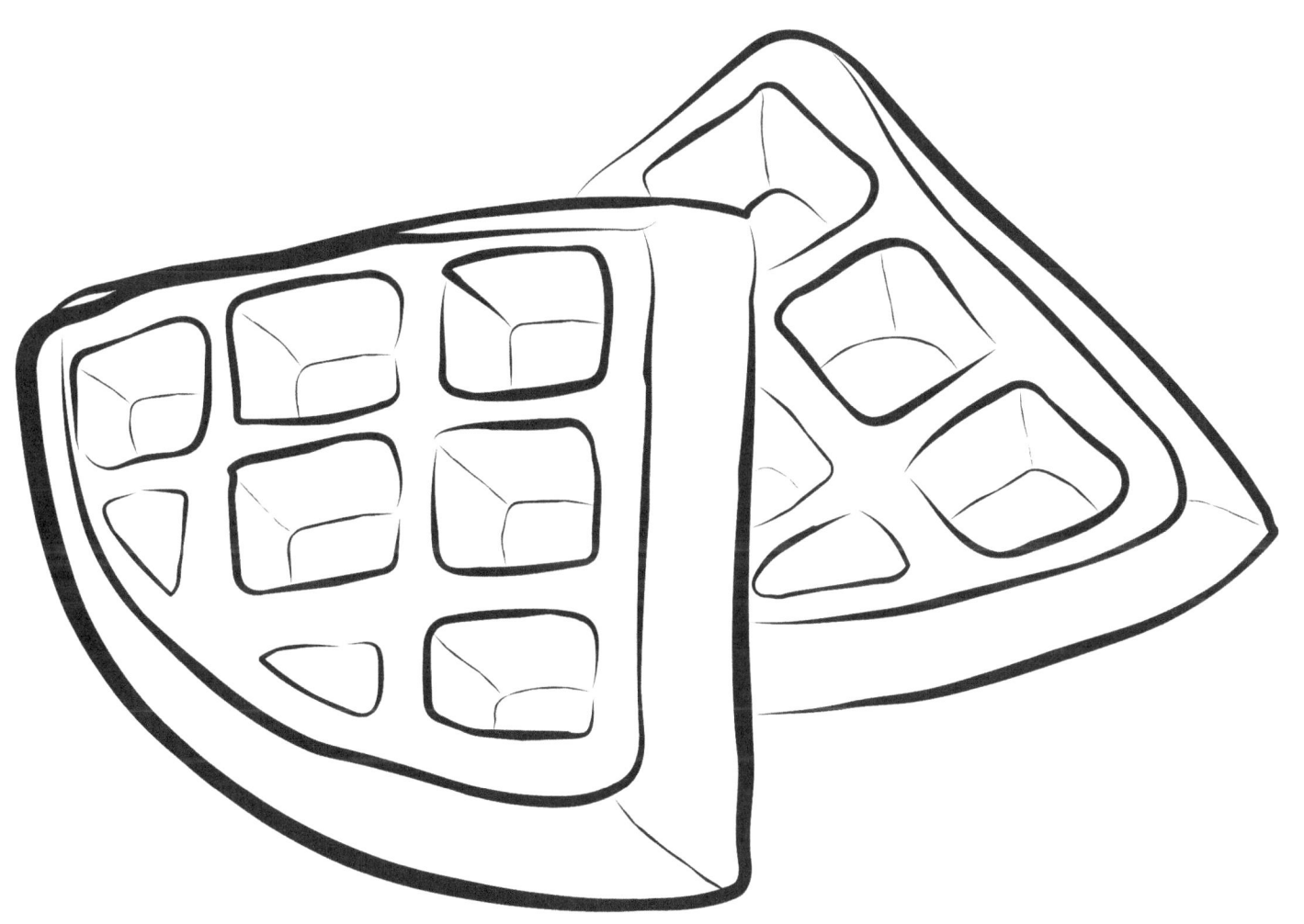

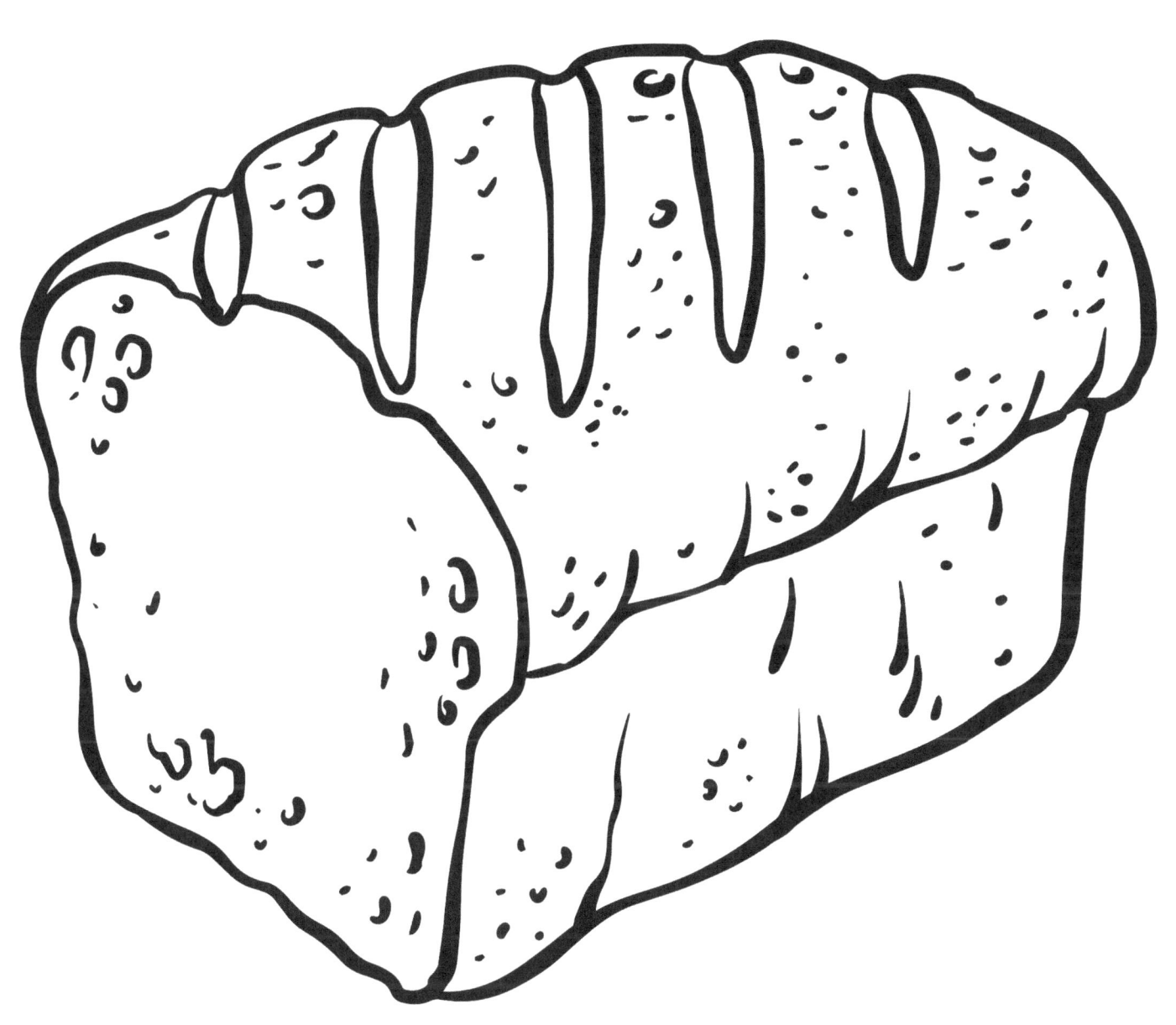

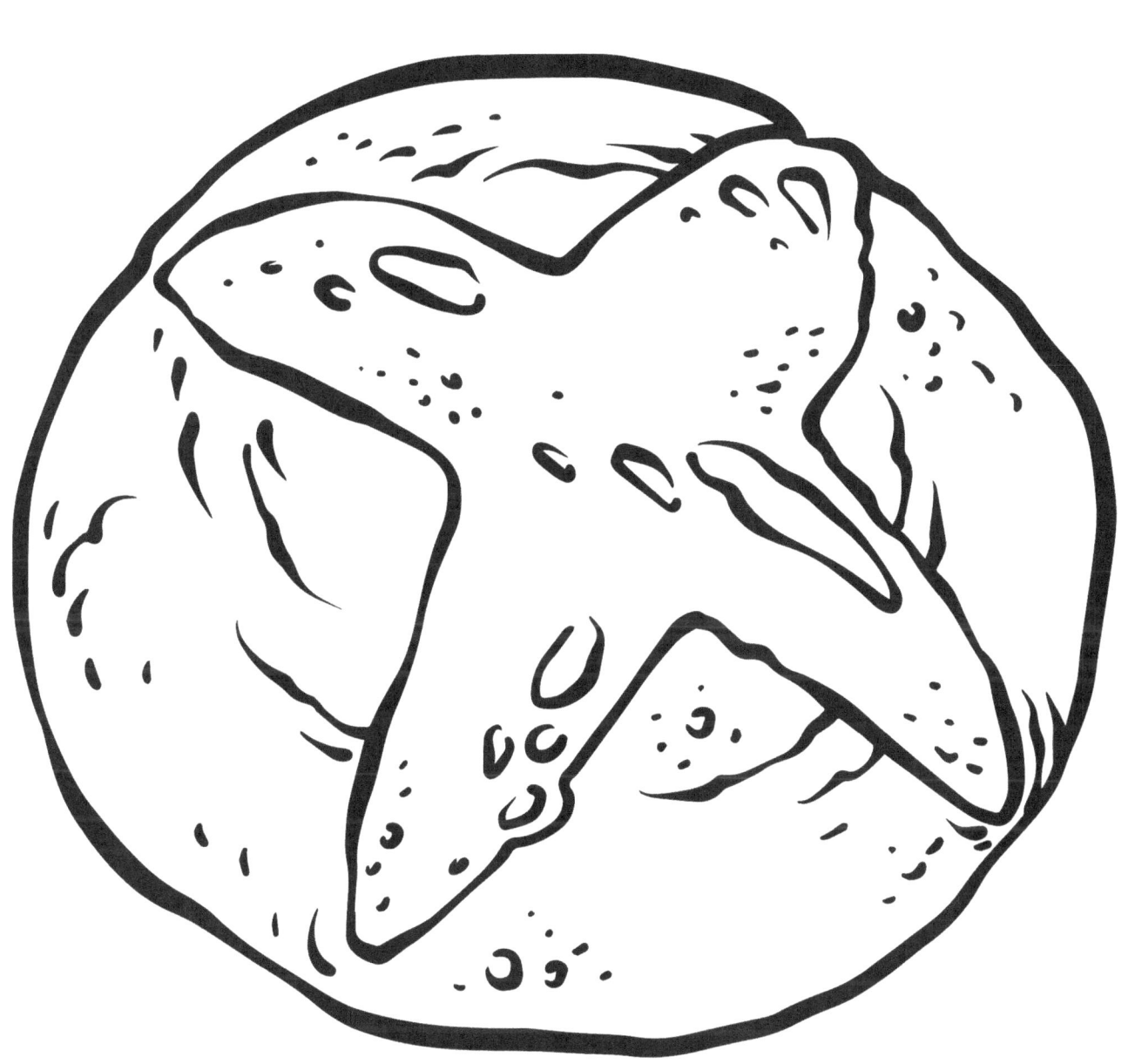

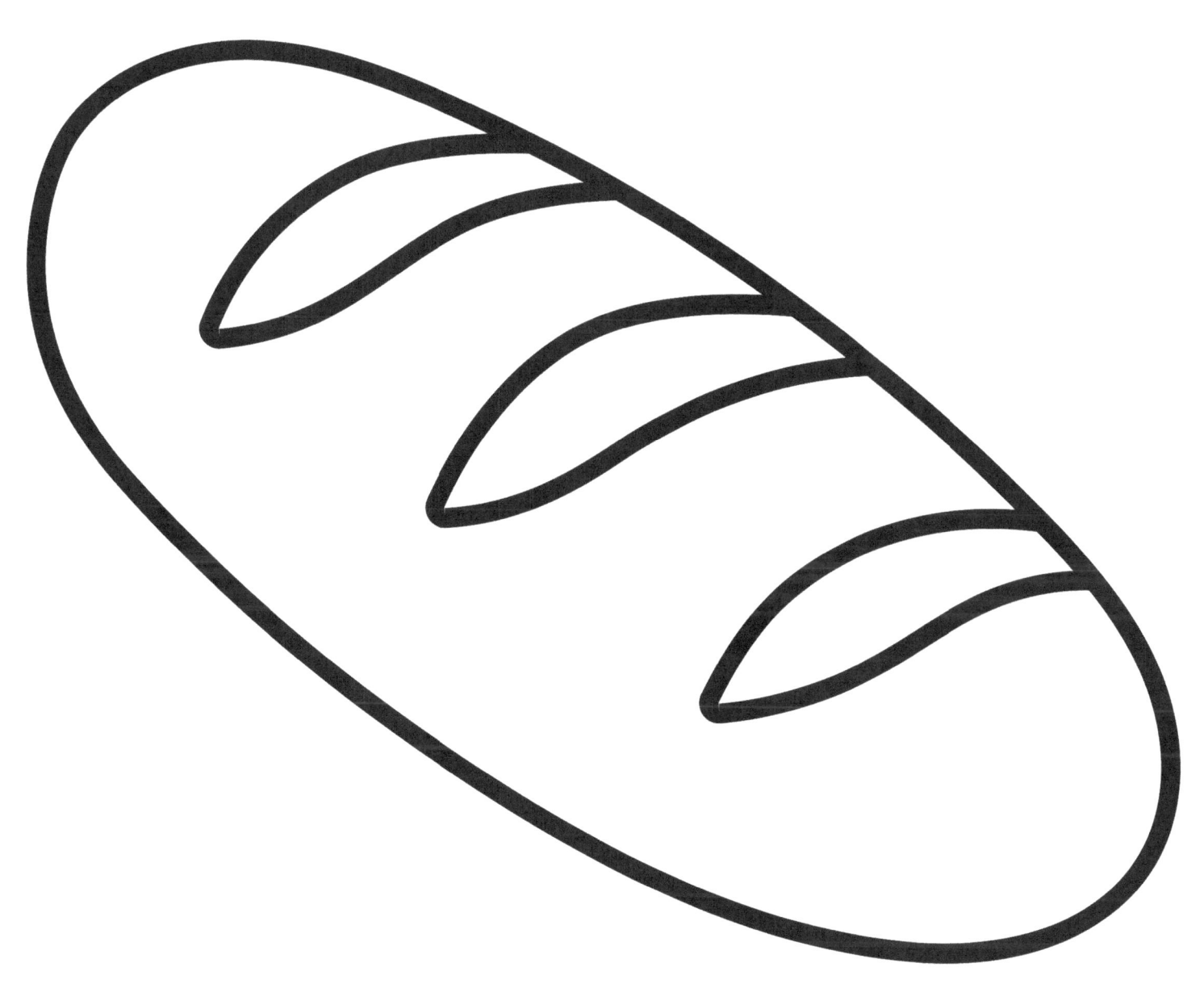

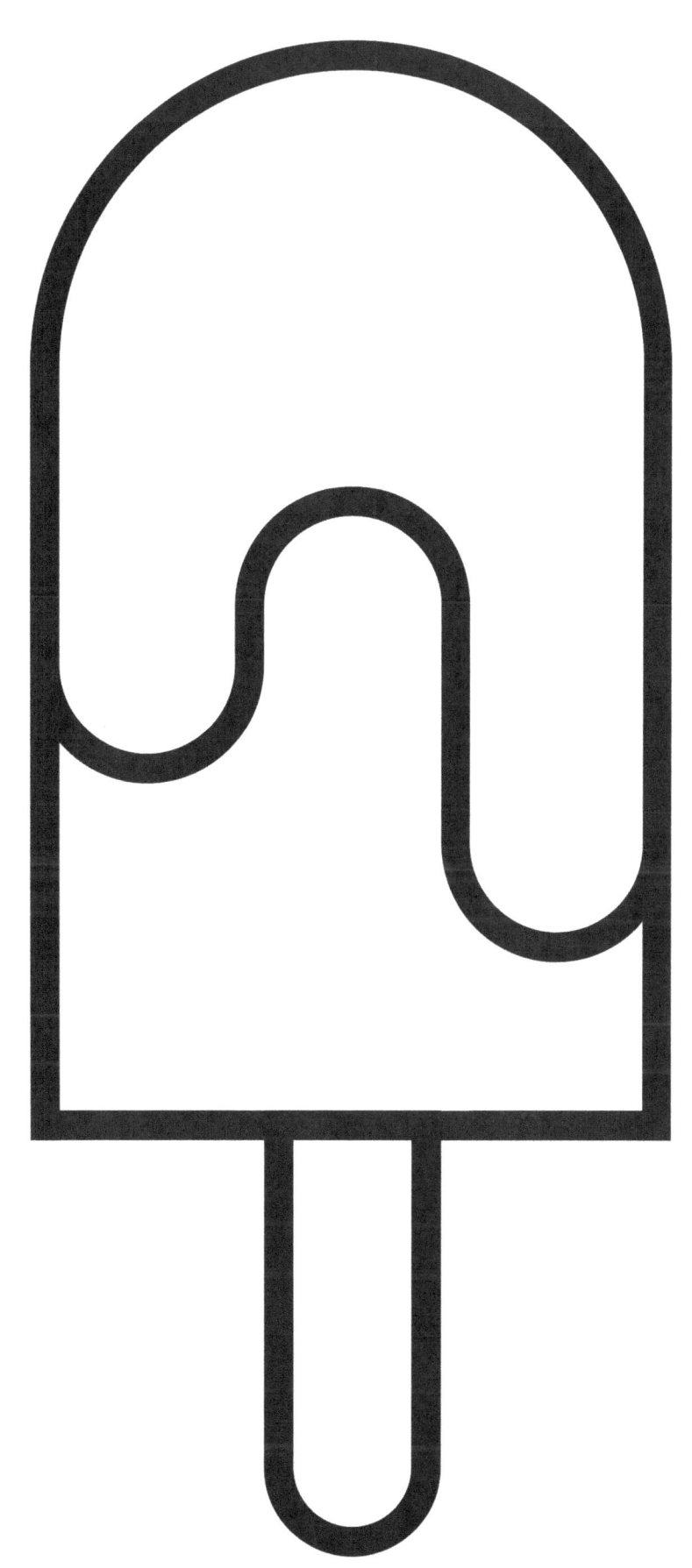

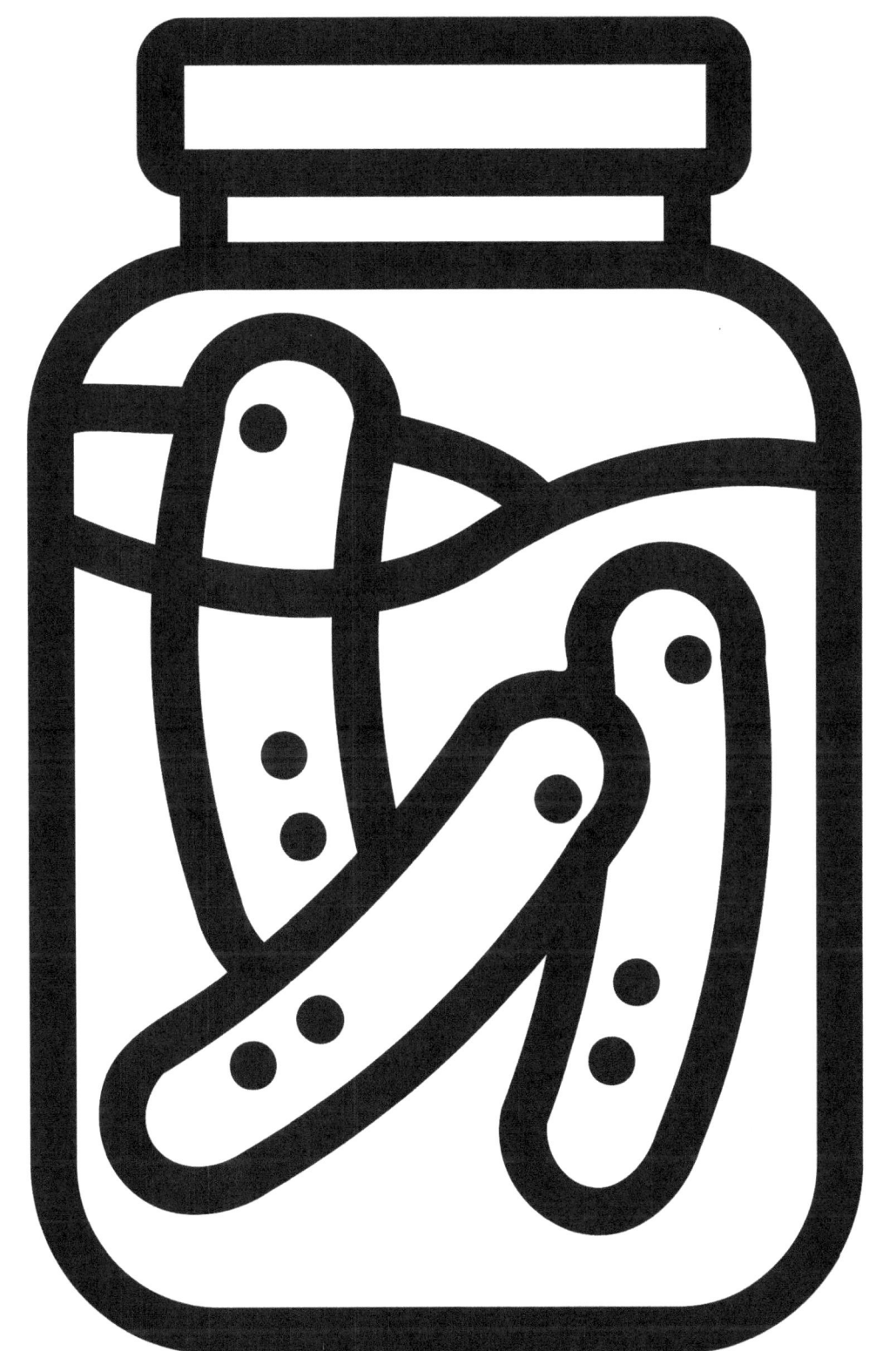

IT'S FACTS TIME!
Let's see if you knew this before

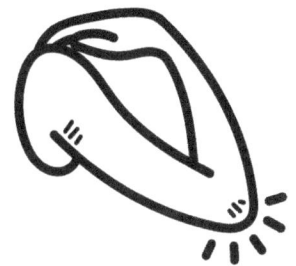

Most people cannot lick their elbows.
(Try it!)

You cannot sneeze with your eyes open.
(Try this too!)

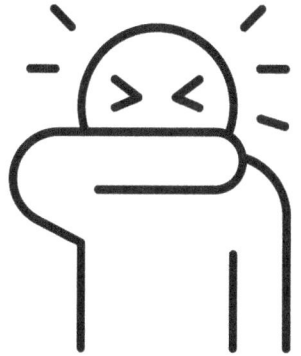

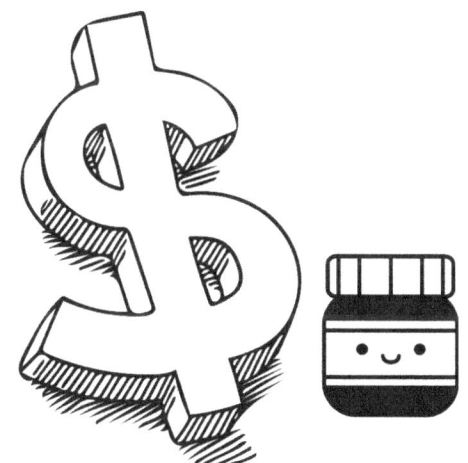

A jar of Nutella is sold every 2.5 seconds.

French fries are Belgian, not French.

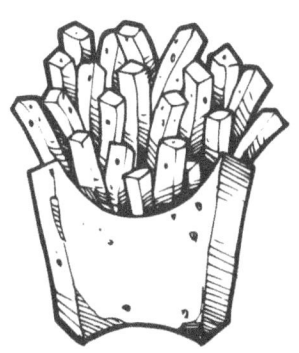

www.ingramcontent.com/pod-product-compliance
Lightning Source LLC
Chambersburg PA
CBHW082343220526
45470CB00008B/2616